THE WELL-STRUCTURED PARAGRAPH

Second Edition

Barbara Williams

Charles E. Merrill Publishing Company
A Bell & Howell Company
Columbus   Toronto   London   Sydney

To
Gerald Warner Brace
with
affection and admiration

Published by
Charles E. Merrill Publishing Company
A Bell & Howell Company
Columbus, Ohio 43216

This book was set in Helios.
The production editor was Elizabeth A. Martin.
The cover was designed by Barbara Davis.
The cover was prepared by Will Chenoweth.

Copyright © 1978, 1970 by Bell & Howell Company. All rights reserved. No part of this book may be reproduced in any form, electronic or mechanical, including photocopy, recording, or any information storage and retrieval system, without permission in writing from the publisher.

Library of Congress Catalog Card Number: 77-23626

International Standard Book Number: 0-675-08429-6

1 2 3 4 5 6 7 8 — 84 83 82 81 80 79 78

Printed in the United States of America

CONTENTS

Preface   v

Part I   Paragraph Elements   1

    Chapter 1   Food for Those Hungry Paragraphs   2
    Chapter 2   Paragraph Unity   5
    Chapter 3   Coherence Through Order and Transition   13

Part II   Methods of Paragraph Development   21

    Chapter 4   Process   23
    Chapter 5   Anecdote (Narration Within Exposition)   27
    Chapter 6   Detail   31
    Chapter 7   Illustration   37
    Chapter 8   Comparison and Contrast   43
    Chapter 9   Analogy   49
    Chapter 10   Analysis   53
    Chapter 11   Definition   57
    Chapter 12   Reasoning   63
    Chapter 13   Combination of Methods   71

Part III   The Whole Composition   75

    Chapter 14   Planning in Advance   76
    Chapter 15   Solving Problems While Writing   85

Part IV   Fundamentals of English Prose   95

    Chapter 16   Glossary of Usage   96
    Chapter 17   Symbols for Correcting Themes   109

Index   131

PREFACE

Most students will never become professional writers, nor do they even aspire to. But they must communicate regularly in writing—with their professors through term papers and essay examinations; with their fellow students through official announcements, committee reports, and articles for campus publications; with businesses and future employers through letters; and even with themselves through classroom notes which they set aside for later reference. The need to master simple expository techniques is therefore as real and immediate to all students as the requirement to study formal rhetoric seems dreary and unreasonable to some. Further discouragement often comes from difficult prose models set up by English teachers of good will, who themselves perceive the best in literature and arbitrarily urge insecure students to emulate the balance of a Woodrow Wilson, the logic of a Paul Tillich, the antithesis of a George Bernard Shaw, or the imagery of a James Joyce. This book, then, operates on the assumption that those students who are intimidated by illustrative material which they cannot understand will more certainly respond to and profit from the competent if not brilliant writing of their peers.

Another assumption, offered more hesitantly, is that some students will develop a degree of self-confidence if encouraged to begin with the shortest expository unit—the paragraph—before attempting a longer composition. The teachers who disagree with me—and I anticipate many—may prefer to assign Part III of this book before Parts I and II. Or they may be willing to consider *Twelve Steps to Better Exposition,* which treats the process of composition more traditionally.

I wish to express my gratitude to Rita Langdon and Frank Fletcher for their helpful suggestions.

PART I

PARAGRAPH ELEMENTS

CHAPTER 1   FOOD FOR THOSE HUNGRY PARAGRAPHS

What do teachers consider the most serious weakness of student composition? Poor spelling? Careless punctuation? Awkward grammar? No. Mechanical errors like these merely slow down communication; they don't usually impede it. But communication will be impeded by two far more serious and far more common problems in student writing: (1) those ideas which are so badly garbled in the process of getting put on paper that they say something very different from what the writer intended, and (2) those ideas which stay forever in the writer's head, never getting put on paper at all.

The first problem—garbled and ambiguous prose—is nearly always the result of fuzzy thinking and therefore is not easily discussed in a textbook. Consequently, the purpose of this book will be to deal with the second problem by showing how to put ideas on paper, or in other words, how to feed the hungry and sickly paragraphs which too frequently occur in student writing. The following example, taken from a freshman theme, is typical:

1. Autonomous centers for black studies should be established on college campuses. This would be an extremely worthwhile project. I feel it is high time that attention be brought to the study of Afro-American history. Blacks have been forced to accept the white man's culture and conform to our rules of society long enough. We have robbed them of their unique and curious ways of life. Their history is an interesting one which is often hidden under the carpet. It cannot be given proper consideration in one or two pages of an American history book. Much can be learned from the hardships of our black brothers. Therefore, I advocate black studies on college campuses.

Whether or not the conclusions expressed by the student writer in the above paragraph are valid, his arguments are not very convincing. Closer inspection reveals that the opinions are feeble because they are starving for some kind of paragraph nourishment: details, examples, anecdotes, analogies, or some other kind of sustenance discussed in

Food for Those Hungry Paragraphs

Part II of this book. None of the sentences in the paragraph above provides any calories, but each is a generalization crying for food:

Autonomous centers for black studies should be established on college campuses.	1st general statement
This would be an extremely worthwhile project.	rephrasing of 1st general statement
I feel it is high time that attention be brought to the study of Afro-American history.	rephrasing of 1st general statement
Blacks have been forced to accept the white man's culture . . .	2nd general statement
. . . and conform to our rules of society long enough.	rephrasing of 2nd general statement
We have robbed them . . .	rephrasing of 2nd general statement
. . . of their unique . . .	3rd general statement
. . . and curious ways of life.	rephrasing of 3rd general statement
Their history is an interesting one . . .	rephrasing of 3rd general statement
. . . which is often hidden under the carpet.	rephrasing of 2nd general statement
It cannot be given proper consideration in one or two pages of an American history book.	4th general statement
Much can be learned from the hardships of our black brothers.	5th general statement
Therefore, I advocate black studies on college campuses.	rephrasing of 1st general statement

In good writing every generalization is vigorous and healthy because it is well fed. But repeating a request for food is not the same thing as providing it. The topic sentence in this paragraph is probably too broad to be proved in a single paragraph, but the student might use the first general statement as the thesis for an entire paper. The

continuous flow [handwritten margin note]

second, third, and fifth general statements could then function as topic sentences for four additional paragraphs, and the fourth general statement might serve as an illustration in support of the second. Probably one or two additional generalizations (with supporting evidence) would provide continuity and depth.

So far we have looked only at broad statements rather than evidence—at generalizations requiring food. What kinds of nourishment can the student writer provide for the hungry mouths which hang gaping? What are some facts, examples, or arguments the student might use?

Or consider another student paragraph:

[2]   American families do not anticipate the problems of aging in either a practical or a humane way. Elderly relatives should be cared for at home, not shipped off to institutions to die among strangers who don't care about them. Everyone will get old in time. Does anyone want to spend his or her final days staring morosely into space and listening to the foolish gibberish of roommates who suffer from mental deterioration? People should plan ahead so they can provide for parents and loved ones at home. In the long run it would be cheaper, too.

Does this paragraph contain any evidence, or is it comprised—like the one which precedes it—of a string of general statements? Have any generalizations been repeated? Could the order of the sentences be improved? Can you see some ways of providing nourishment for the opinions expressed here? Does the paragraph contain too many opinions to be treated in a single paragraph?

Part II of this book will suggest specific methods for the care and feeding of paragraphs, but before looking at them, you may find it useful to learn more about paragraph anatomy. Chapters 2 and 3 will describe this interesting organism, the paragraph.

[Handwritten notes at top:]
Unity = write about the topic sentence.
Coherence = Use adequate transitions - are the clue - to stitch them together.
② Sentences must be in logical order.
Main idea = Thesis.
Exposition - narration
argument - Description

CHAPTER 2   PARAGRAPH UNITY

Most of the writing you will do in college will be explanation—how Shakespeare's "Hamlet" reflects English rather than Danish society, how the various courts of law function within our democratic system, what adaptations mammals have made in their evolution from life in the sea. In this kind of writing, known technically as *exposition,* your purpose is to enlarge the reader's understanding of something by sharing your own knowledge. Because exposition *explains,* it always provides both information and value judgments. It differs, therefore, (1) from news reporting, which *informs* only (without value judgments or opinions), (2) from narration, which *shows* human beings acting out events (without an obvious overriding judgment), and (3) from description, which *details* the physical properties of something (with or without any statement of opinion). <u>Within these four kinds of prose—exposition, news reporting, narration, and description—the paragraph has different functions and different structures, as shown in the chart on page 6.</u>

In exposition, each paragraph must explain an idea. And because a sentence or two can seldom explain anything, most expository paragraphs should consist of three or more supporting sentences plus a topic sentence which summarizes them. The paragraph below illustrates the typical expository arrangement with the topic sentence at the beginning: **TOPIC SENTENCE**

     The age at which a youngster may be safely given a .22 should not be determined by chronological age but by physical strength and sense of responsibility. It is dangerous to place a gun in the hands of a youngster who cannot handle it with ease; for unless the rifle can be held properly for sighting and the trigger squeezed steadily, shots can go anywhere. Also, it should be understood that pranks and carelessness have no place in hunting or on the shooting range. Anyone who does not realize how important are the   [3] rules for gun owners—and when left alone will do something foolish like shooting lizards on the ground at close range—is not ready for the experience of owning a gun. Regardless of age, the youngster must first demonstrate in other aspects of his or her life a willingness to heed the advice of someone with training and experience.

Kind of Paragraphs	Purpose of Paragraphs	Length of Paragraphs	Content of Paragraphs	Special Qualities of Whole Composition
Expository	Signifies a logical unit.	Fairly consistent throughout composition (about 100–200 words). Shorter paragraphs used sparingly and only for (1) transition, (2) summary, (3) emphasis.	Topic sentence (or central idea) plus specific evidence in three or more supporting sentences.	Composition calls for logical arrangement with introduction, body, conclusion.
Narrative	Signifies a unit of the story or a change of the speaker in dialogue.	Very short to very long.	No topic sentence required because . . .	. . . material calls for time order, not logical order.
Descriptive	Signifies a unit of details.	Fairly consistent throughout composition.	Topic sentence seldom required because . . .	. . . material conveys feelings or sensory impressions. Details often call for space order, seldom for logical order.
argumentative Newspaper	Provides eye appeal for fast reading.	Very short. One or two sentences.	Facts only. No topic sentence. No opinion.	First paragraph provides all essential information. Subsequent paragraphs decrease in order of importance. No conclusion. Note: Editorials and most columns do contain opinions and follow the rules for exposition, except that paragraphs are shorter.

Although you may place the topic sentence anywhere within a paragraph (and even omit it after you gain experience as a writer), you will probably find that a well-worded summary placed at the beginning will help you write a better paragraph. But to be well worded a topic sentence should not try to cover too much. Of course any topic sentence is a general statement, but a good one also focuses on one

Paragraph Unity

small aspect of the material through special *key words.* These key words represent the *controlling idea* because they control what part of the topic sentence you must emphasize in the paragraph.

In illustration ③ above, the key words are *strength* and *responsibility.* Notice how the writer has developed the controlling idea as the paragraph moves forward. The concept of *strength* is defined as being able to hold [the] rifle properly for sighting and to squeeze the trigger steadily. The concept of responsibility is defined as acting wisely without supervision and heeding advice. A less important controlling idea, *chronological age,* is returned to in the final sentence of the paragraph.

By setting down a controlling idea and then focusing carefully on it, the student has written a unified paragraph in which all of the sentences work toward the same purpose. On the other hand, clumsy and disunified paragraphs will usually result from topic sentences which contain no controlling ideas or from topic sentences which contain accidental controlling ideas. Contrast paragraph ③ with the disunified paragraphs, ④ and ⑤ :

CONTROLLING IDEA

④

I enjoy all kinds of sports. When I first entered high school, I was a fat, soft little kid who didn't know much about the game of football. All I knew was I wanted to play. I wasn't the best kid who had ever tried out for the Highland team, but I was willing to try. After three months of hard effort, I made the team. I started out as a fullback and then became a kicker. The coaches didn't always like my form, but I didn't like their suggestions too well either.

Poor—No Controlling Idea

"I enjoy all kinds of sports" would make only a fair thesis statement (see p. 77) for an entire theme. Certainly it is too broad an idea to serve as the topic sentence for a single paragraph. It needs a sharper focus through the use of a controlling idea, such as "I enjoy sports when I don't have to worry about *form*"—or even better—"I enjoy *football kicking* when I don't have to worry about *form.*" Because the writer has no controlling idea, all kinds of unrelated information are introduced.

⑤

Today many organizations are being formed in order to help unstable and insecure young people who have turned to barbiturates and other drugs. But everyone must be open-minded and help one another. No one can sit back and let a few do the task. Many people have learned about the consequences of drug abuse through schools, families, and friends. Yet when some parents are told their children are involved with drugs, they become angry and refuse to face facts.

Poor—Unheeded Controlling Idea

Although the student writer has set down a controlling idea—organizations—that idea has not been discussed. Nowhere else in the paragraph are organizations referred to again, possibly because the writer has no information on the subject. One clue that the writer lacks knowledge is the condescending tone used. It is always easier to advise someone to do something than to give any reasons, facts, or examples. Consequently, poorly-informed people will often try to substitute preaching for explaining.

The Well-Structured Paragraph

Whatever other qualities they possess, expository paragraphs must have unity—that is, each paragraph must develop one idea and one idea only. Following these rules will help achieve paragraph unity:

1. Begin each main paragraph with a topic sentence or a transition sentence (See p. 91) followed by a topic sentence.
2. Focus the topic sentence on one aspect of a problem by means of key words (controlling idea).
3. Support the controlling idea in three or more concrete sentences.
4. Use short paragraphs of one, two, or three sentences sparingly and only for (a) transition, (b) summary, or (c) emphasis.

Study the following paragraphs to decide if they are unified or disunified and why.

6. Dating by computer can be much more humorous and exciting than most people realize. Potential customers often look upon the service as formidable and nauseating. When the idea of match-making by machine was first conceived, it was intended to help people who had limited opportunities to meet members of the opposite sex or who had difficulty in appraising other people after one or two encounters. But if looked at in a strictly practical way, computerized dating can save both time and money.

7. Are today's highways more hazardous than the highways of yesterday? Some people believe that accidents would not happen if we had good highways, but engineers know that good highways alone won't prevent accidents unless they are used by good drivers. When drivers really learn to look out for the other person, our highway fatalities will cease to occur. One place drivers must learn to watch out for the other guy is in getting on the freeway. Drivers don't watch the speed of other cars and try to keep up so the other cars don't have to slow down. Accidents are not caused by highways or by poorly constructed cars but by people.

EXERCISE A

In the blank after each topic sentence below, write the word or words which express the controlling idea.

1. Despite increasing divorce rates, people need lasting relationships.

2. Wife beating occurs in all levels of society.

3. The scientific method as we know it is only 350 years old.

4. No one watches a poor figure skater.

5. Women's sports are more interesting to watch than men's.

6. By our standards, nineteenth century historians were naive.

7. The "Sons of Liberty" were once the hoodlums of colonial Boston.

8. A university is only as good as its library.

9. Millions of children will go to bed hungry tonight.

10. Erratic weather would pose fewer hazards if the world weren't overpopulated.

11. The fifty-five miles per hour speed limit causes more problems than it solves.

12. Many men judge other men by what their wives look like.

13. Manners have disappeared from Western society.

14. Since the Watergate era, leadership is evaluated in terms of credibility rather than accomplishment.

15. Intellectual growth is easier than emotional growth.

EXERCISE B

Writing Topic Sentences

For each of the subjects below write a topic sentence and underline its controlling idea.

1. Phobias

2. Alcoholism

3. Genealogy

4. Astrology

Paragraph Unity

5. Antiques

6. Earthquakes, floods, or other natural disasters

7. Meaningless rituals

8. Bumper stickers

9. Status license plates

CHAPTER 3   COHERENCE THROUGH ORDER AND TRANSITION

Next to unity, the most important quality of an expository paragraph is *coherence,* which literally means "the ability to stick together." For not only should every sentence in the paragraph discuss the same controlling idea, but each sentence should also connect smoothly to the sentence which precedes it and the one which follows. Such coherence is achieved by two necessary techniques, which work together:

1. the logical arrangement of material,
2. the use of transitional devices (words, phrases, or even sentences that act as bridges between ideas).

PARAGRAPH ORDER

Among the many ways in which to arrange material, the following are probably the most common:

1. time order—details arranged chronologically (first to last)
2. space order—details arranged by spatial relationship (left to right, right to left, near to far, far to near, low to high, high to low)

13

3. climactic (or emphatic) order—details arranged by importance (least important to most important)
4. order of complexity—details arranged by difficulty (least difficult to most difficult)
5. cause to effect order—details arranged by causal relationship (A causes B)
6. effect to cause order (B is caused by A)

TIME ORDER

Material for at least three kinds of paragraphs falls naturally into time order: historical discussions, narratives (including anecdotes), and process explanations. Both historical discussions and narratives relate their details according to what happened first. Similarly, process paragraphs provide sets of instructions for the reader according to what steps he or she must follow first. Such instructions might explain, for instance, how to tie a dry fly, how to make crepe paper roses, how to maneuver a glider behind an airplane tow, or how to prepare mock turtle soup. The writer must explain the steps in the order that they take place, or the reader will become thoroughly confused.

Because time order is an obvious method of arrangement, students often apply it in situations where chronology is awkward. For example, a theme entitled "Problems with the College Pass-Fail System" should not begin "When I was a senior in high school. . . ." And even narrative papers should focus on the important events rather than minor chronological details. Therefore, a student who wants to explain an exciting afternoon surfing experience will not begin by saying "Mother called me for breakfast at 7:30 in the morning. . . ."

Before deciding to use time order, you should consider two questions: (1) Is chronology important to the material, or are ideas the principal concerns? (2) What elements of chronology are important to the central purpose, and which ones are unnecessary and dull? Chapters 4 and 5 provide examples for appropriate use of time order in paragraph development.

SPACE ORDER

The physical appearance of something—an old man, a mountain lake, a mortuary room, a modern apartment building—usually calls for the organization of details into some kind of spatial relationship. For instance, you might describe the old man from his head to his feet. Or you might describe the mountain scene from left to right, or near to far. Space order—once you get the principles in mind—is fairly easy to write but is seldom useful beyond a paragraph or two within a large expository composition.

CLIMACTIC (OR EMPHATIC) ORDER

Climactic order is by far the most versatile and effective method of expository arrangement. Used not only within paragraphs but within sentences and entire compositions, this arrangement of material is not difficult to master *and indeed may be the most valuable technique of writing that you will ever learn.* It simply means taking advantage of the fact that the reader remembers best the material which appears last. The following paragraph illustrates the climactic method

Coherence Through Order and Transition

by listing the details about William McGuffey's academic life in ascending order:

> When William Holmes McGuffey was appointed president of Ohio University in 1839, he was six days short of his thirty-ninth birthday. But already he was far more serious and already he had acquired far more academic honors than most men twice his age. He had been teaching professionally since he was twelve. He had tutored and reared a younger brother. He had taught at Miami University and served as president of Cincinnati College. And he had written the incredibly popular McGuffey Eclectic Readers, which eventually were to become the nation's number two best-seller, only after the Bible itself.

ORDER OF COMPLEXITY

Closely resembling climactic order, the order of complexity begins with easy or familiar examples and works up to difficult ones. It proves extremely useful when you must explain complicated material to the reader.

CAUSE TO EFFECT AND EFFECT TO CAUSE ORDER

Argumentative or other explanatory paragraphs will often trace the relationship between a cause and its effect. This kind of arrangement is, of course, comparable to arrangement of material by time order because a sequence of events is involved in both. (For examples of cause to effect and effect to cause paragraphs, see pp. 66–67).

TRANSITIONAL DEVICES

Despite its importance, the logical arrangement of material will not hold a paragraph together without assistance from certain mechanical aids, known more specifically as *transitional devices.* These include the following:

1. transitional words and phrases
2. repetition of key terms
3. synonyms and other substitutes
4. pronouns
5. parallel constructions

COMMON TRANSITIONAL WORDS AND PHRASES

The following words and phrases are used to make a qualification or contrast:

on the other hand	perhaps	over the years
nevertheless	but	formerly
still	or	recently
unfortunately	nor	lately
despite	yet	today
although	so	apparently
on the contrary	when	whenever
by contrast	after	meanwhile
however	because	
since	long ago	

to introduce an illustration:

thus	for instance	namely
for example	to illustrate	according to

to add a thought:

in addition	likewise
moreover	again
next	similarly
second	furthermore
in the second place	

to indicate a conclusion or result:

therefore	to conclude	to summarize
as a result	in conclusion	in summary
consequently	finally	
accordingly	thus	
in other words	then	
to sum up	hence	

The paragraph below demonstrates how stilted and cumbersome prose sounds when it lacks adequate transitions. Although the material is clear, unified, and well arranged, the composition does not flow as smoothly as it should.

9   Many stories both fanciful and factual have connected the creatures of nature with weather prediction. The most common myth is the one about the groundhog, who comes out from his den at noon on February 2, to look for his shadow. If he sees his reflection, cold weather will continue for another six weeks. If he does not, spring will appear immediately. The groundhog tells us nothing about weather. The story concerning him is an unreliable superstition. A chirping cricket does signal a rise in temperature by rubbing his forewings together more quickly. By adding thirty-seven to the number of chirps a cricket makes in fifteen seconds, a person can fairly accurately determine the temperature.

However, the addition of a few simple transitional words and phrases not only improves the cadence of the passage but even helps clarify the meaning by providing bridges between ideas.

Coherence Through Order and Transition

Over the years many stories both fanciful and factual have connected the creatures of nature with weather prediction. *Perhaps* the most common myth is the one about the groundhog, who *according to tradition* comes out from his den at noon on February 2, to look for his shadow. If he sees his reflection, cold weather will continue for another six weeks, *but* if he does not, spring will appear immediately. *Unfortunately, however,* the groundhog tells us nothing about weather, *for* the story concerning him is an unreliable superstition. *On the other hand,* a chirping cricket does signal a rise in temperature by rubbing his forewings together more quickly. By adding thirty-seven to the number of chirps a cricket makes in fifteen seconds, a person can fairly accurately determine the temperature.

|10|

From past experience you have probably observed that thoughtless repetition is tiresome—even annoying. But repetition of those key words which carry essential meaning adds to the clarity and coherence of prose. Notice how frequently certain terms are repeated in the paragraph below:

REPETITION OF KEY TERMS

The conflict between two utterly opposing *views* on education rages on. One *view*, represented by followers of Maria Montessori, says that children should be trained on a prekindergarten level to develop their sense perception and coordination so that they can learn to *read* at an early age. The other *view* insists that children should not be encouraged to *read* until they are physically ready, often well after the age of seven. Moreover, to substantiate their claim, persons who hold to this second *view* will sometimes cite the educational experience of *Woodrow Wilson*, who later was to become one of the most brilliant men ever to participate in American public life. Young *Wilson* was not enrolled in school until after the Civil War ended, when he was nine. Being a slow learner, he could not *read* with ease until he was eleven. Nevertheless, by the time he received his Ph.D. from Johns Hopkins University, *Wilson* had caught up with and surpassed in academic achievements nearly all the men his age who had begun their schooling much earlier.

|11|

But not every key term can be repeated endlessly. The writer of the paragraph above has also used substitute expressions for some of the key terms.

SYNONYMS AND OTHER SUBSTITUTES

Key Term	**Substitutes**
education	trained
	develop
	learn
	educational experience
	school
	academic achievements
	schooling
Woodrow Wilson	one of the most brilliant men
	a slow learner

Word substitutes must, of course, be natural and not call attention to themselves. Prose which reaches for phony circumlocutions like *encounter the dark charioteer, join the choir invisible, pay the debt to nature, escape to a lovelier realm, launch off to eternity,* or *meet the grim reaper* to avoid the straightforward word *death* makes an honest reader squirm.

Prounoun substitutes for key words can also help connect sentences together.

PRONOUNS

The Well-Structured Paragraph

[12]   Because *its body* is supported by water, the blue whale can grow to a size considerably larger than any land animal ever discovered. Even larger than the great dinosaurs which once roamed our planet, *it* commonly grows as long as 100 feet and as heavy as 150 tons. *It* is propelled through the water by a horizontal tail which provides the momentum for the creature to leap completely out of the water or dive straight down in the sea to a depth of 2,000 feet. The size of a newborn blue whale is more or less dependent upon the size of *its* mother, but *some* have been recorded up to twenty-five feet and eight tons, more than twice as big as a full-grown elephant.

Teachers are often reluctant to encourage students to use pronouns for transitions because inexperienced writers, as a rule, are inclined to use too many pronouns rather than too few and frequently commit grammatical errors in the process. (See p. 110) Whenever using a pronoun, therefore, you should consciously remind yourself of what noun that pronoun is standing in for and make certain that the two words agree in person, number, and gender.

PARALLELISM

The repetition of grammatical constructions not only lends rhythm and balance to prose but also provides skillful transitions. Two kinds of parallelism occur in paragraph [13]. The second sentence demonstrates a rather common method of setting down items in a series in parallel form. But the extended parallelism in the next three sentences is more unusual and more effective. Notice that the sentences proceed in climactic order, stating the most important idea last.

[13]   American political life in the early twentieth century was ▬▬▬ general reform movement which stemmed from both major parties. ▬▬▬ the cry of "progress," Democrats and Republicans alike introduced laws to control food and drugs, regulate public banking, recognize labor unions, provide revenue through a federal income tax, and eliminate child labor and sweatshops. The goal of these reformers was nothing more radical than to make the pursuit of happiness a meaningful possibility for all Americans. Their method was to make government a vital instrument for that purpose. And their faith was to see that it could and would be done.

This last paragraph [13] is an example of successful prose because it makes good use of the two principles for achieving coherence:

1. the logical arrangement of material (in this instance, climactic order),
2. the use of transitional devices (in this instance, parallelism).

EXERCISE A

Climactic Order

Arrange the following groups of sentences into climactic order. Put a **1** before the topic sentence, which summarizes everything else. Then number the supporting sentences in ascending order, leaving the most important or most complicated idea until the end.

1. _(5) 2_ The federal government should impose much more rigid safety requirements on all vehicles.
   _3_ The police should patrol the highways more vigorously.
   _1_ Highway safety can be improved in four ways.
   _(2) 4_ Dangerous stretches of highway should be closed to the public.
   _(4) 5_ The states should establish higher requirements for drivers' licenses.

2. _2_ The governor, who was a member of the Church of England, insisted the Puritans observe Christmas Day, which they considered a pagan holiday.
   _3_ Rumors were spreading of a witchcraft conspiracy in Salem Village.
   _1_ The years between 1684 and 1692 brought so many troubles to their world that the Puritans of New England believed the devil was striving to make as many converts as possible before the millenium, due about 1700.
   _4_ The people learned that an earthquake, undoubtedly caused by the devil, had killed nearly 2,000 persons in Jamaica.
   _6_ The French and Indians were making new attacks on the frontier settlements.
   _5_ They suspected the governor of entering into unholy alliances with the Indians.

3. _____ Vaccines provide some immunity.
   _____ It is imperative that patients be kept in absolute isolation.
   _____ Waste materials must be burned or treated with a strong disinfectant.
   _____ Whenever possible, control of flies and insects is helpful.
   _1_ During a cholera epidemic, strict sanitary measures must be observed.
   _____ Bacteria must be destroyed by sterilizing water, pasteurizing milk, and cooking all food.

4. _____ Some researchers believe that most human communication is nonverbal.
   _____ Dance therapists believe that a patient's movements reflect both personality and emotional health.
   _____ It is usually easier for a patient to conceal attitudes in verbal communication than in physical movement.
   _____ Many of the exercises are designed to help patients discover feelings about which their minds are unaware.
   _____ The main advantage of dance therapy is that the patient's improvement can be readily observed.
   _____ Mental health therapists are discovering many ways that dance exercises can be used in diagnosing and treating emotionally disturbed patients.

EXERCISE B

Transitional Devices

The paragraph below achieves coherence through a variety of transitional devices.

During those early days after World War II there were many other couples who could not afford automobiles and therefore relied on bicycles to get them to and from their offices and classrooms. But my husband and I were probably the only husband-wife team who shared a one-seater, second-hand bicycle along the cobblestone streets of Cambridge. In a way, it was painful, sharing that bicycle. It was painful receiving the jests and stares of pedestrians. And it was painful in a well-localized portion of my anatomy, as anyone who has seen those cobblestones may suspect. However, no real process of learning is achieved without some pain—if only the small torment of giving up old prejudices.

1. List all the words and phrases used for transition _____

2. How many times are the following key terms used?

   cobblestone(s) _____

   bicycle(s) _____

   painful _____

3. What substitutes can you find for the following key terms?

   couples _____

   pain _____

6. In the first sentence, what pronouns are used to refer to the noun *couples*? _____

5. What three sentences rely on parallel construction to hold them together? _____

6. How many different transitional devices can you find in the last sentence to make it cohere to the sentence which precedes it? _____ List them _____

PART II

METHODS OF PARAGRAPH DEVELOPMENT

CHAPTER 4　PROCESS

Of the various kinds of expository paragraphs, the easiest to write is the one which discusses a process. The reason for this is that while material for other kinds of paragraphs may suggest several logical methods of arrangement, the stages of a process always call for chronological order. In other words, you must describe the steps in the order that they take place.

Process paragraphs are of two kinds: how-to-do-it and process explanation.

HOW-TO-DO-IT PARAGRAPHS

The first kind of process paragraph instructs the reader on how to do something: how to make a floral arrangement, how to tune a guitar, how to play ice hockey, how to prune an apricot tree, or—as in paragraph 14 —how to administer mouth-to-mouth artificial respiration:

14 Once you encounter a person who has stopped breathing, you should begin immediately to follow the procedures for mouth-to-mouth breathing, the method of artificial respiration recommended by the U.S. Army, the American Red Cross, and the Boy Scouts of America. First, place the victim on his back and remove any foreign matter from his mouth with your fingers or a cloth wrapped around them. Then tilt his head backwards so that his chin is pointing up. Next, pull his mouth open and his jaw forward, depressing his tongue firmly with your thumb. With your free hand, pinch his nostrils shut to prevent the air which you blow into his mouth from escaping through his nose. Then place your mouth tightly over the victim's if he is an adult. If he is a small child, place your mouth over both his mouth and nose. Blow into his mouth until you see his chest rise. Then turn your head to the side and listen for the out-rush of air which indicates an air exchange. Repeat the process. For an adult, blow vigorously about twelve times a minute. For a small child, blow less vigorously and at the rate of about twenty times a minute. If you are not getting an air exchange, recheck the victim's mouth for foreign matter as well as the position of his head. Then begin blowing again. When the victim begins to breathe for himself, continue blowing, timing your efforts to coincide with his own. After his breathing becomes strong, keep him horizontal and cover him with a blanket or coat. Call a doctor immediately.

[15] Sometimes such a set of instructions will be written for a limited group of readers already familiar with the equipment required:

> When bridling and saddling a horse, you must make certain that the tack fits properly. A loose bridle will prevent you from controlling the animal properly. However, a tight bridle and saddle will cause pain and possibly even face and back sores. Always work from the left side of the horse. First, slip the reins over the head and neck so you will have some slight control while you remove the halter. Then, holding the bridle in your right hand and the bit in your left, slip the bit into its mouth and work the crown over its ears and into position. Buckle the throatlatch so that the bit rides just at the corners of the horse's mouth. Don't use the reins to tie the horse while you get your saddle, but snap a cross-tie into a bit ring if the animal won't stand still. Although English saddles do not require a pad, a western saddle calls for a blanket or pad which first must be smoothed out. Next, place the saddle on the horse's back so that it rests comfortably forward. Fasten the strap just tight enough for you barely to slip your fingers underneath. Finally, adjust the stirrups so that they fit to your armpit when your arm and fingers are extended to the stirrup catch on the saddle.

More often, however, you should assume that the reader has had no previous experience and carefully list near the beginning of the set of instructions all the materials needed.

[16] Before you can hold an old-fashioned clambake you must first do some sleuthing to discover what beaches permit fires and if special licenses are required. Once that matter is settled, you must plan ample marketing time, probably the day before your clambake. From the market you will need the following: steamer clams (allow six to eight per person and be careful to select fresh ones without a "fishy" odor), lobsters, fresh corn, potatoes, lemons, butter (allow at least one pound for every six people), rolls, paper plates, plastic knives and forks, paper napkins (three or more per person), soda pop, and some kind of dessert. At home after your marketing, you must then scrub the potatoes and remove the silk but not the husks from the corn. Then round up the other things you must take to the beach: a large barrel or garbage can (clean, please) for your oven, a lid and/or heavy parchment paper, a shovel, asbestos gloves, buckets or wheelbarrows for transporting rocks and seaweed, matches, firewood, salt and pepper, a pan for melting the butter, and ice chests with ice for the soda pop. As soon as you arrive at the beach, start a roaring fire and collect big rocks to put in it. While the rocks are heating through, dig a hole in the sand large enough for the barrel or garbage can. Then collect plenty of wet seaweed. Into the barrel place the following in layers: seaweed, hot rocks, seaweed, lobster, seaweed, hot rocks, seaweed, potatoes, seaweed, hot rocks, seaweed, corn, seaweed, hot rocks, seaweed, clams, seaweed, hot rocks, seaweed, parchment (or lid), and sand. Leave your "oven" for four to five hours until clams on top are steamy. Melt butter and cut lemons into wedges to serve with the seafood. The red roe (or eggs) you may find in your clams are edible. So is the green liver on the inside. The only part you won't want to eat is the digestive sac under the eyes.

Unfortunately, the writers of how-to-do-it paragraphs too often assume that their readers know as much about their subjects as they do. Obviously, it is always better to give too many instructions than too few and to put them carefully in the exact order.

PROCESS EXPLANATION

The second kind of process paragraph tells how something is currently done or how it was done in the past: how copper is separated

Process

from other minerals by the flotation process, how frontiersmen made their own lead balls, or—as in paragraph [17]—how ancient Indians produced pottery over the years:

[17] During the time of the pit-house villages—roughly A.D. 300—the Indians of Mesa Verde discovered that their native clay would make pottery containers vastly superior to baskets, for they did not leak, they could not be gnawed by field mice, and they could be placed directly over fire for cooking purposes. The earliest potters demonstrated little skill. Their thick and uneven jars were not fired but left to harden in the sun. Such clumsy vessels were heavy to carry and therefore mainly used to store the corn the Indians would need in colder seasons or times of famine. Later, the potters started firing their bowls and jars, and finally they developed the thin and beautifully decorated wares for which Mesa Verde is famous. The designs on the pottery from this late period were skillfully painted, always in black. To obtain the paint, the potters boiled the tender shoots of the common beeweed until a thick, brown liquid appeared. They applied the brown paint with brushes made from yucca fibers, and when the pottery was fired, the brown designs turned black.

Occasionally a paragraph describes a process which exists in theory but has never been proved in actual fact:

[18] Early Marxists set forth five steps whereby communists could speed up the overthrow of capitalism. Stirring up class and racial conflict would be the starting point. Catching capitalism at a weak point, communists would then foment a revolutionary outbreak, bringing the old order down by force and violence. The postrevolutionary government would be dictatorship—in theory, dictatorship of the working class. The next step would be the nationalism of property as socialism replaced capitalism. Then as all remaining elements of selfishness and class spirit disappeared, the socialist state would evolve into the final stages of communism where the state would wither away and people would live by the rule, "From each according to his ability, to each according to his need."

Although process paragraphs are fairly easy to write, they have a limited application in exposition. You should, of course, be able to recognize them and to write them when necessary, but mastering the other techniques of paragraph development described hereafter will be more valuable.

EXERCISE A

Beginning with (1) a topic sentence and (2) a list of materials required, write a how-to-do-it paragraph of at least 150 words on one of the following:

How to make paper flowers
How to set up a compost pile
How to travel with children
How to get ready for a pack hike
How to set up a butterfly collection
How to build a bird house
How to construct a loom
How to make sourdough biscuits
How to perform some scientific experiment
How to make a candle
How to select a guitar

How to clean a revolver
How to get rid of a garden pest
How to take an essay examination
How to sell a magazine subscription
How to hunt for fossils
How to plan a birthday party
How to make a pin-hole camera
How to set up an aquarium or terrarium
How to perform some magic trick
How to select a used car
How to make a collage

EXERCISE B

Beginning with a topic sentence, write a process explanation (not a story) of at least 150 words explaining one of the following:

A holiday celebration at your house
A community festival
Indian sand painting or other primitive art
Planning a display
Planning a panel discussion
Planning a wedding ceremony
Tapestry weaving or some other medieval craft
The construction of a bridge, dam, subway, or famous building

CHAPTER 5   ANECDOTE (Narration Within Exposition)

Despite the fact that storytelling is narration rather than exposition, you may choose to relate a very brief incident, or anecdote, to illustrate a topic sentence. Such a narrative therefore has an expository purpose because it helps to develop a central idea. Notice the topic sentence in paragraph [19]. It not only states the central idea (*people are imitative*) but announces how the student will prove that idea (through material about *annual spring clean-up campaigns*). The fact that the writer plans to tell us a story, however, is not indicated until the third sentence.

[19] The annual spring clean-up campaigns sponsored in cities throughout the nation clearly prove how imitative people are. They all began in 1909 in Cleveland, Ohio, because one sad-eyed little girl regularly showed up for school with a dirty face, tangled hair, and the same grimy blouse and skirt. Day after day the teacher watched the child, her heart aching for the pitiful creature growing up in misery and neglect. Finally the teacher decided to do the best she could. She presented her pupil with a gift—a bright blue pinafore—which so delighted the girl that she came to school the next day with a shiny face and glistening hair. And soon a change came over the child's family. Noticing her daughter's beautiful appearance, the mother started setting the table with a cloth and scrubbing her floors. And the father started removing the weeds and debris from their yard. At length the neighbors caught the spirit, too, and began cleaning their yards and painting their houses. Reports of the neighborhood clean-up spread through Cleveland and even as far away as Cincinnati. Four years later, in 1913, the whole city of Cincinnati sponsored the country's first organized clean-up campaign. So one little girl's blue pinafore was the beginning of an annual nationwide movement.

Logically, a topic sentence can appear before, after, or even in the middle of the anecdote. But the most common procedure is to place the summary statement at the beginning of the paragraph, as in paragraph [20]:

20 American tourists who scorn the usual commercial hotels and restaurants to mingle among the natives of foreign countries must either develop strong stomachs or run the risk of jeopardizing international relations. Upon returning home, two Americans reported a traumatic experience they endured as guests in the Chinese backwoods. Seated at the dinner table one evening, they observed their host masking a proud smile as a servant carried in a large green tray. With a flourish the waiter put the tray on a small serving table and then set before each diner a small covered bowl. When the Americans removed the lids from their bowls, they discovered that the main course consisted of a dish full of brown, hard-shelled bugs about one and one-fourth inches long. They were all wriggling their numerous legs and wiry antennae and acting very much alive.

Like process paragraphs, anecdotes are fairly easy to write because they, too, have an underlying structure based upon time order, or a sequence of events. The details of Captain Cook's adventures in the Hawaiian Islands naturally fall into the chronological arrangement which the writer has used in paragraph **21** :

21 Primitive people interpret nearly every unusual phenomenon in terms of religion or superstition, often with unfortunate results. So it was that when Captain Cook landed on the Hawaiian Islands, the natives, who had never seen a white man before, quite naturally assumed that he was a god of some kind. On his first visit to the Islands, the natives treated Cook with great reverence and lavished gifts upon him. But when he returned to the Islands the following year, the tribesmen became suspicious. Cook was unable to display the talent of healing which the Islanders believed a god should have. And when his men provoked a quarrel with some of the local warriors, the Englishmen seemed rather human after all. The natives attacked Cook and his men, killing the famous Pacific Ocean explorer.

Time is the underlying structure of all narratives—short stories, novels, plays, movies, television dramas. Always there exists a chronological order in which the events took place, even though the author of a long narrative may deliberately violate the correct sequence by means of a dramatic technique known as *flashback*. An anecdotal paragraph used to illustrate an expository idea is much too brief to allow for effective use of flashback, however. You must be careful, therefore, to keep the details of your anecdote in their precise sequence in order to avoid confusing your reader.

Other problems sometimes occur with the use of anecdotes. Because public speakers realize how effective a good story can be, they will often look for their anecdotes first and then try to weave a speech around them. Unfortunately, this tail-wagging approach can lead to difficulty in serious written composition. Exposition is concerned with ideas—not merely with entertaining an audience—and techniques which work for after dinner speakers may seem shallow and fuzzy-minded when committed to paper. In serious expository composition you should use only those anecdotes which illustrate significant points, and you should keep them brief enough so they won't distract from the main purpose of your paper. On the whole, however, the use of anecdotes will be pleasant for both you and the reader.

EXERCISE

Beginning with a topic sentence, write an anecdotal paragraph of at least 100 words which illustrates one of the following points:

Men are more vain than women (or vice versa)
College students are sometimes more absent-minded than their professors
Poor handwriting can get you into trouble
Rebellion doesn't always bring happiness
Dogs are not man's best friend
People enjoy being fooled
Gum chewing can be as expensive as smoking
Children are not always a blessing
Knowledge is not always power
Communication is more difficult than you might think
Sunday is seldom a day of rest
Pleasure seeking is not always pleasant
My mother (father, boy friend, etc.) has a strange habit
Tyranny can victimize the tyrant
Living in the future can jeopardize the happiness of the moment

CHAPTER 6   DETAIL

At this point in the study of the paragraph, you have already learned that the main thing which separates effective composition from weak and listless prose is the command of detail which the writer demonstrates in supporting topic sentences. Why, then, do students so often produce meaningless paragraphs instead of lively and informative ones? Two possible answers occur: (1) the students don't know enough about the subjects on which they are writing, and (2) they don't know the difference between details and generalizations.

Overcoming the first hurdle—lack of information—is simple. By consulting one or two brief library sources or by interviewing someone with firsthand experience, you should be able to gather adequate material to write an interesting, factual paper on any theme topic which an English composition instructor is likely to assign. (Long research papers represent another kind of approach, of course, not considered here.) However, overcoming the second hurdle—inability to differentiate between details and generalizations—requires the development of a new skill.

By definition, details are facts or particulars. They are more exact and more easily demonstrated to another person than are generalizations, which are large propositions or conclusions.

22   As opposed to the modern-day games for athletes of both sexes, the first Olympics in ancient Greece weren't games at all. They were contests to teach young men the skills of war. Players raced against each other because running was important in ancient warfare. They wrestled each other, usually until one wrestler was seriously hurt. They showed their strength by throwing heavy metal objects like the discus and the javelin. But they didn't play any ball games.

The topic idea in paragraph **22** above does not appear in a single topic sentence but in the first two and last sentence in the paragraph. Notice that these sentences are somewhat vague and cannot be visualized as easily as the sentences in the middle of the paragraph which contain the supporting details. Likewise, the details in paragraph **23** are physical qualities visible to the human eye:

23   One of England's most famous furniture designers of the late Georgian period was a former preacher, Thomas Sheraton, who gave his name to a distinct style. Working primarily with mahogany, satinwood, and rosewood, Sheraton designed furniture which looked fragile but actually was very strong. The backs of his chairs consisted of four-sided frames and central splats, the latter usually decorated with urns or lyres. The legs of his chairs were slender and tapered, often with six to eight sides. Famous for his exquisite sideboards and writing desks, which were as practical as they were attractive, Sheraton decorated his furniture with inlays and bandings of unusual woods. He was fond of delicate relief carvings and also less commonly ornamented his furniture with painted flowers and scrolls.

Sometimes, however, details are not seen by the eye but are perceived by the mind after wide experience or wide reading. For an example of this kind of detail, see the paragraph below:

24   It is in the New Testament that the familiar Christian concept of Satan really developed. There Satan took on terrible qualities that had never been attributed to him before. He was described as all-powerful, exerting far greater control over people than previously supposed. He was seen as the force in the universe opposite to God, the symbol of all hate and evil, and the author of every misfortune. According to one student of the Bible, the early Christian priests made up stories about Satan's wickedness in order to contrast God's greatness, and they overemphasized his importance in order to frighten the people into doing good. The Devil therefore became a scapegoat upon whom the common man could blame his own weaknesses and sins. In the process, the Old Testament "accuser" grew into the vile "tempter" who terrifies twentieth century Christians.

Notice from paragraphs **22** , **23** ,and **24** that details may be either tangible or intangible. But they will always be single parts which make up some larger whole. In paragraph **25** , the writer assembles many kinds of details or facts which he could not have observed firsthand. Rather, his information represents the observations of several researchers over a period of years.

Detail

[25] Once used in the United States only by people from low-income groups, marijuana is now commonly smoked by members of the armed forces, students in ivy league colleges, and teenagers from upper middle class neighborhoods. Various studies estimate twenty million users in this country, mostly under twenty-five years of age. And despite warnings from parents, educators, and professional organizations, the number of marijuana users continues to rise. More than 30 percent of the American college students polled in one nationwide survey reported having used marijuana at least once. Half of those students admitted to having used the drug two or more times.

The use of concrete detail is the most fundamental method of developing topic sentences. While reading about the other kinds of paragraph development in subsequent chapters of this book, notice how many of them are dependent upon the careful marshalling of such facts, or particulars.

EXERCISE

Beginning with a topic sentence, write a paragraph of at least 100 words which develops one of the subjects below through the use of detail:

Requirements for some job, profession, or sport
Causes of industrial accidents
Causes of accidents in the home
Symptoms of some mental or physical disease
Qualities of a good play, book, movie, newspaper, or magazine
Qualities of an effective leader or effective teacher
Crime in your city, state, or country
Wildflowers or animals in a region you know
Space exploration in the 1980s
Transportation in the 1880s
Sunday afternoon at Coney Island, Disneyland, or similar resort
Monday morning at police headquarters, the state legislature, or business office you are familiar with
Sunday morning in a specific church
Saturday night at a specific bar or discotheque

CHAPTER 7 ILLUSTRATION

Weary of the unsupported generalizations in a student theme, a freshman composition teacher once wrote the following comment in large red letters across the top of the first page:

Revise this paper, carefully illustrating the topic sentences I have underlined.

But she was thoroughly abashed when the student's revision was submitted, looking in part like this:

Many dissidents think only of destroying the Establishment's form of government.

However, other dissidents want to correct the problems in our society and thus preserve our way of life.

Obviously, the teacher had falsely assumed that her students knew the difference between a drawing and a prose illustration, the latter being an example (or several examples) to explain or illuminate a rhetorical point in question. Prose illustrations may call for a fairly detailed anecdote extending to a paragraph or more (See Chapter 5), or they may require three or four very brief narratives, as in paragraph 26:

26   In the early days of the city, the Puritans of Boston used their Common as both a jail and a place of execution. The first man to be placed in the stocks on Boston Common was the carpenter who built them. His Puritan neighbors decided he had charged too much for his labor and promptly dealt with his obvious ungodliness. Later, a sailor who had just arrived home after being at sea for three years was whipped on the Common for kissing his wife in public on Sunday. But the flogging worked too well, for the next year he had to be punished for ignoring her. More desperate criminals were hanged from a big elm tree on the Common. These included several women, one of whom had stolen a bonnet. Another lady was hanged as a witch. She had made the mistake of curing sick friends with her herbs and homemade broth.

By reducing the narrative element in each example, you can crowd still greater numbers of illustrations into a single paragraph:

27   And what were the fearful men of this country doing during those early years after the depression of 1929? Some were organizing communist cells in government agencies, labor unions, colleges, businesses, and farm organizations. Some were following Huey Long and Father Coughlin, with their slick solutions for desperate ills. Others were refusing to engage in any forward-looking activity, preferring to grumble about their bad luck and to pine for the "good old days." Still others were seeking emotional comfort in quoting Herbert Spencer against the Wagner Act, Social Security, and the Tennessee Valley Authority and applying to F.D.R. the same off-color political jokes that have been used against every reasonably effective president since George Washington.

Likewise, the student writer of paragraph 28 uses several different illustrations to prove her topic sentence at the beginning:

28   Although we often think of primitive Indians as being nomadic and warlike, they taught us many things about living in a peaceful world. It was not until Europeans saw how the Indians made rubber that white men acquired such useful items as elastic bands, erasers, hot water bottles, gym shoes, boots, and automobile tires. The hammock is another invention that we owe the Indian. This wonderful kind of bed was unknown in Europe before Columbus came to America and is one of several ideas the Indians gave to us about the use of ropes and baskets. They also taught us how to put sponges in clay pots to make them stronger and how to raise crops by irrigation. They showed us more than 200 kinds of potatoes and introduced many new crops, including beans, peanuts, sunflowers, cacao, tomatoes, and the Jerusalem artichoke. Although the white Europeans already grew corn to feed to their pigs and cows, the Indians taught them many ways to use this plant for human consumption. In addition to growing plants, the Indians taught them about raising honey bees, the llama, the alpaca, the muskduck, and the turkey as food sources.

The examples in paragraphs 26, 27, and 28 are skeletal stories which could be, if the writers wishes, expanded into much longer anecdotes. Similarly, the examples in paragraph 29 could be recounted as lengthy narratives. However, the student writer has chosen to imply the stories rather than to tell them, so that what remains is nothing more than a list:

Illustration

The targets of the right wing from 100 years ago to the present time have included a curious list of human beings, concepts, government institutions, and even mythical characters: Catholics, Englishmen, Italians, Poles, Jews, Zionism, the liquor trade, the League of Nations, the United Nations, UNICEF, the Red Cross, the teaching of evolution, psychiatrists, mental health clinics, government regulation of business, the TVA, the federal income tax, Franklin D. Roosevelt, General George Marshall, social security, Medicare, fluoridation, synthetic vitamins, the Supreme Court, Earl Warren, the State Department, peaceful co-existence, blacks, the National Association for the Advancement of Colored People, Martin Luther King, rock-and-roll music, Dwight D. Eisenhower, the Eastern Establishment, ivy league colleges, even Mary Poppins and Santa Claus (for what could be more frightening than a foreigner who maneuvers in space or a give-away artist in a red suit!).

Most illustrative material will contain some kind of story, either stated or implied. This narrative quality is one thing that distinguishes illustration from detail. Another difference helpful to remember is that although illustration (example) usually incorporates detail (basic facts), detail cannot incorporate illustration. But the most important difference is that details are single parts of a whole whereas illustrations exist independently.

Don't be concerned if you cannot readily distinguish between detail and illustration. The important thing to remember is that both methods are specific, informative, and extremely useful in expository writing. Furthermore, well-selected illustrations are easy to understand and are interesting both to writer and reader.

EXERCISE

Beginning with a topic sentence, write a paragraph of at least 100 words developed by illustration on one of the subjects below:

People are too suspicious of each other
People are not wary enough of each other
Animals are suspicious of people
People are suspicious of animals
Etiquette is common sense
Etiquette is not based on common sense
Problems in college registration
Problems in voter registration
Problems in financing national elections
Problems in student elections
The wrong people run for office
Religious or racial prejudice
Causes of panic
Good bargains
Bad bargains
Mistakes in choosing dates or marriage partners
Dreams
Suicide
Superstition
Misconceptions about rape
Fortune telling
Family relations
Consulting a psychiatrist

CHAPTER 8   COMPARISON AND CONTRAST

Nearly always when lining up two or more things for discussion, you will both compare (point out their similarities) and contrast (point out their differences). The technique of comparison and contrast is a highly useful one which forces you to think in concrete terms and therefore is usually interesting. It may extend throughout a long composition or remain in a much shorter unit—possibly a single sentence. Paragraph 30 illustrates comparison and contrast:

Comparison Contrast	At first glance the scientist's reproductions of the ancient mastodon look very much like our modern-day elephant: the same sturdy legs, the same long trunk, the same huge ears. But closer inspection reveals some differences between the prehistoric creature and the modern one. The mastodon was covered with long, heavy hair. It was shorter and stockier than its modern cousin. And its longer tusks curved up more at the ends. Some mastodons even had four tusks in contrast to the elephant's two.	30

Most paragraphs developed by comparison and contrast will discuss only a pair of objects, opinions, or people rather than three or more. And they will probably use one of two methods. The first method examines one half of the pair in detail before moving to the other half, as in paragraph 31 below:

  Byzantine art	Before about 1300 A.D., Italian painters followed the Byzantine style of art, named after the capital city of the Eastern Roman Empire. This artistic style made use of unrealistic human figures, stiffly posed and elaborately draped. Flat colors with little shadowing were set against gold backgrounds and ornate physical objects such as	31

The Well-Structured Paragraph

Renaissance art

chairs. But gradually in the fourteenth century and after, Italian artists began introducing the changes which would later characterize the Renaissance style. Human figures became more lifelike in shape and gesture. Colors became realistic. Solid yellow backgrounds were replaced by landscapes and bits of architecture with depth and shading. In time, portraiture became highly developed, and artists struggled to reproduce the distinctive characteristics of their subjects.

The other common method of developing by comparison and contrast looks at both members of the pair at once, discussing the material about them point by point:

32

Parentage

Appearance

Character

Ambition
Influence

Reputation

Like Lincoln, William McGuffey had been born to poor parents—a father with little ambition other than to hunt, a mother who taught her children the scriptures and dreamed of their future success. Like Lincoln, he was tall, rawboned, strong, and homely. Like Lincoln, he was obedient, responsible, and hard working. Like Lincoln, he thirsted for knowledge and was known to walk miles to borrow any kind of book. Like Lincoln, he was to influence the pattern of nineteenth century American thought. But unlike Lincoln, he was not to be remembered and loved as a person long after his death.

Such a point-by-point examination may rely on both comparison and contrast or only one:

33

Topic sentence

Parentage

Education

Employment

Hitler, rather than Mussolini, rose to greater heights of villainy, perhaps because the forces which shaped him were more traumatic and kept the mainspring of his character wound more taut. The parents of Mussolini were undistinguished but conventional—a village blacksmith and a country schoolmistress. But Hitler's father was even more dour and unconventional than the strange Austrian peasants among whom he lived. Although Mussolini was expelled for bad conduct from the strict friars' school where he was sent as a boy, he did eventually graduate from normal school and obtained his credentials to become a teacher. But Hitler was never able to listen to any teacher who presumed to know more than he. He dropped out of high school before taking his final examinations and thereafter failed twice in his attempts to enter the academy of Fine Arts in Vienna. Whereas Mussolini went on to become a fairly competent teacher and newspaper editor, Hitler never succeeded at any profession outside war and politics. Barely able to support himself at a variety of jobs, Hitler blamed the rest of the world for his failures, focusing his scorn on the wealthy and influential Jews.

But the two methods of comparison and contrast illustrated in paragraphs 31 , 32 and 33 in no way represent all the possibilities. Occasionally, for instance, one thing will be described by comparing it to many other things. In paragraph 34 , the writer tells us that violent death from a nuclear bomb is really not very different from violent death from a number of other sources:

But for the individual *as an individual,* is the issue of the nuclear bomb really different from the problem of violent death which has confronted men of all ages? Is the Chinese bomb any different from, any deadlier than, Socrates' hemlock? Would it be any more painful than Jesus' cross? Would it be more individually searing than the fire at Joan of Arc's feet? Would it be any more decapitating than the blade which ended the life of Sir Thomas More? Would it be any more fatal than well-aimed muskets across a Lexington Common? And would it really, for an individual, be any more frightening than a Japanese Kamikaze plane coming straight at him on a World War II flattop? 34

In addition, you may find many other ways of arranging material for comparison and contrast.

EXERCISE

Beginning with a topic sentence, write a paragraph of at least 125 words which develops one of the subjects below through the use of comparison and contrast:

Camping vs. luxury travel
Air vs. ground travel
Speed reading vs. leisurely reading
Ballet vs. modern dance
Military draft vs. volunteer army
Two wars in U.S. history
Two methods of taxation
Liberal arts education vs. trade school education
Two historical figures
Two characters from fiction, TV, or comic strips
Two newspaper columnists
Two famous sports personalities
Two famous entertainers
Two political candidates
Two religions or churches
Two members of your family
Two of your friends
Your attitudes five years ago and today
Naturopathy vs. medicine
The I.R.A. and the P.L.O.
Two theories of education
Two theories of psychotherapy
Sex attitudes in two specific countries
Penal systems in two specific countries

EXERCISE

Beginning with a topic sentence, write a paragraph of at least 125 words which develops one of the subjects below through the use of comparison and contrast:

Camping vs. luxury travel
Air vs. ground travel
Speed reading vs. leisurely reading
Ballet vs. modern dance
Military draft vs. volunteer army
Two wars in U.S. history
Two methods of taxation
Liberal arts education vs. trade school education
Two historical figures
Two characters from fiction, TV, or comic strips
Two newspaper columnists
Two famous sports personalities
Two famous entertainers
Two political candidates
Two religions or churches
Two members of your family
Two of your friends
Your attitudes five years ago and today
Naturopathy vs. medicine
The I.R.A. and the P.L.O.
Two theories of education
Two theories of psychotherapy
Sex attitudes in two specific countries
Penal systems in two specific countries

CHAPTER 9   ANALOGY

A comparison between two things which are basically different but which have similar qualities is called an analogy. Unlike the method of paragraph development discussed in chapter 8, however, analogy is seldom concerned with contrasts—only with points of similarity. Its main purpose is to explain something which is unfamiliar by comparing it to something which is readily understood. Therefore, as in the three paragraphs which follow, analogy frequently discusses an abstract idea by comparing it to an object which the reader has seen, touched, smelled, heard, or tasted.

Paragraph 35 discusses democracy in terms of something most people have seen—at least from a distance:

> As Fisher Ames of the Jeffersonian era once put it, "Democracy is like a raft. You never sink, but damn it, your feet are always in the water." Our raft today is tossed by waves of communism abroad, poverty and racial strife at home, and general stupidity and carelessness. We might wish for a calmer sea and a steadier vessel. But we cannot improve our lot by capsizing the raft, or throwing ourselves or some other travelers into the water, or cutting loose the anchor or mast, or even painting slogans on the sail. [35]

The writer of paragraph 36 also discusses an abstract idea in terms of something concrete, comparing one aspect of democracy to something which everyone can reproduce in the imagination from a combination of actual and photographic experiences:

> Government service is like an unscaled mountain range which challenges the vigorous and responsible climber. But the ascent can never be made by the lazy or indifferent—only by men and women with two kinds of capacity about them. First, they must have a kind of far-distance vision which enables them to identify every peak in the range: labor-management negotiations which do not overlook the public interest, social acceptance and economic opportunity for blacks, Indians, and other minority peoples, development and wise management of the country's water and land resources, rising living [36]

standards, peace, and justice for all people throughout the world. Second, the men and women in public service should have the mountain climber's determination to conquer every height.

Paragraph 37 differs from paragraphs 35 and 36 in that its comparison is in smaller detail. Rather than viewing a raft or mountain from a distance, the analogy looks through an imaginary magnifying glass to compare the tiny fibers of a tapestry to the structure of American freedom:

37 The structure of free American society can be compared to the warp and woof of a tapestry. Central to the whole fabric—or the woof thread of our liberty—is the Constitution upon which everything else depends. But intertwined with it are at least three colorful warp threads. The first is the freedom to be insecure, for in Benjamin Franklin's words, "Those who would sacrifice a little liberty for temporary safety deserve neither liberty nor safety." The second is the freedom for unpopular thought, which results in the diversity of opinion necessary to democracy. The third is the freedom to preserve freedom—that is, the responsibilities of citizenship which each individual must bear. And like the constitutional woof, the warp threads must be strong, or rents in the whole fabric will occur.

Occasionally an analogy will compare two things with which the reader is only vaguely familiar. However, by visualizing them in relationship to each other, he or she gains a better understanding of both. The next paragraph paraphrases Winston Churchill's comparison of an army general and a landscape painter. Although you may have no personal knowledge of the requirements of either profession, Churchill's analogy provides explanation on a concrete level:

38 According to Winston Churchill, the painter of a picture, like the commander-in-chief of an army, must first devise a plan of action and second maintain a strategic reserve. In order to accomplish the first, both the artist and the general will thoroughly scout the regions where the battles are to be undertaken. They will then study the accomplishments of the successful officers of the past to compare them to their own firsthand observations. Nevertheless, it is the skill in withholding their reserves which will probably determine whether both the general and the painter will achieve success. To the painter the reserves consist of proportion, or the techniques by which he expresses the relationship of light and dark, near and far, up and down.*

Useful as it can be when properly employed, analogy is not easy to write. And it has logical limitations as well. Inasmuch as the two things being compared will always be dissimilar in some major aspect, an analogy will never resolve an argument. Because termites destroy foundations of buildings does not prove that the National States' Rights Party will destroy America. Because pornography is becoming easily accessible does not prove that we will meet the same fate as the Roman Empire. Because one falling domino can knock down several more in a line does not prove that communism must be contained. In other words, although a conclusion may be true, it is never the analogy which makes it true.

Use analogies only to explain something the reader may not understand, never to prove a point of view.

---

*Winston Churchill, *Amid These Storms* (New York: Charles Scribner's Sons, 1932).

EXERCISE

Beginning with a topic sentence, write a paragraph of at least 125 words which explains one of the following abstractions by comparing it to something the reader has seen, felt, heard, smelled, or tasted:

Feminine liberation	Male chauvinism
Urban renewal	Library research
Censorship	Communism
Fascism	Socialism
Free enterprise	Transcendental meditation
Mysticism	Death
Birth	Slavery
War	Divorce
Marriage	Senility
Adolescence	Bigotry
Neurosis	Psychosis
Prostitution	Depression
Anger	

CHAPTER 10 ANALYSIS

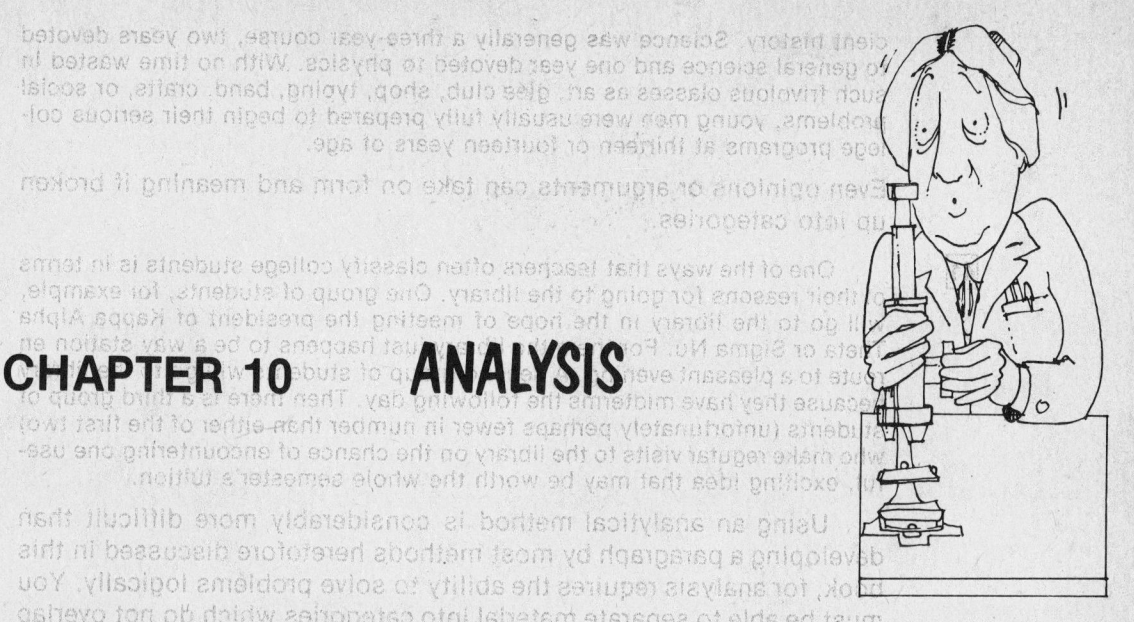

Coming from the Greek word for "a breaking up," *analysis* means to divide something into elements which can be studied separately. A technical piece of machinery, for instance, is best understood if considered in terms of three or four major sections or functions.

A firearm of any size consists of four main parts: (1) barrel, (2) chamber, (3) breech mechanism, and (4) firing mechanism. The barrel is a long tube which may be smooth, as in a shotgun, or may be spirally grooved on its inner surface, as in a rifle. At the rear of the barrel is a widened hole, or chamber, which holds the cartridge, or explosive charge. Farther still to the rear is the breech mechanism, which holds the cartridge in place and closes the end of the barrel. The firing mechanism varies widely in large and small arms but often consists of a spring which drives a pointed firing pin against a primer in the cartridge. [39]

Likewise, with a great deal of information to present on some relatively abstract subject, you may find it useful to divide material into several major categories. Confronted with a wealth of detail about college preparatory education in the 1800s, the student writer of paragraph [40] arranged his information according to classroom subjects which nineteenth century pupils were obliged to study.

A hundred and fifty years ago no American girls and few of this country's boys went to college, but those young men who did hope eventually to become doctors, lawyers, teachers, or ministers began studying at seven or eight years of age to develop skills in five general subjects: English, foreign languages, mathematics, history, and science. The study of English frequently required six years, during which time the pupils were constantly drilled in spelling, punctuation, parts of speech, and grammar. A thorough knowledge of Latin grammar was also required, and to gain proficiency to pass their college entrance examinations most boys studied the language for five or six years. In addition, they took three or four years of French and another two or three years of German or Greek. Like English, mathematics often required six years of study, but history usually took only four—two years of American history, one year of English history, and one year of an- [40]

cient history. Science was generally a three-year course, two years devoted to general science and one year devoted to physics. With no time wasted in such frivolous classes as art, glee club, shop, typing, band, crafts, or social problems, young men were usually fully prepared to begin their serious college programs at thirteen or fourteen years of age.

Even opinions or arguments can take on form and meaning if broken up into categories.

41   One of the ways that teachers often classify college students is in terms of their reasons for going to the library. One group of students, for example, will go to the library in the hope of meeting the president of Kappa Alpha Theta or Sigma Nu. For them the library just happens to be a way station en route to a pleasant evening. A second group of students will go to the library because they have midterms the following day. Then there is a third group of students (unfortunately perhaps fewer in number than either of the first two) who make regular visits to the library on the chance of encountering one useful, exciting idea that may be worth the whole semester's tuition.

Using an analytical method is considerably more difficult than developing a paragraph by most methods heretofore discussed in this book, for analysis requires the ability to solve problems logically. You must be able to separate material into categories which do not overlap each other, as they do in the first list below:

Overlapping Categories
1. Competitive Sports
   A. Team Sports
   B. Individual Sports
   C. Baseball
   D. Soccer
   E. Gymnastics
   F. Golf
   G. Football
   H. Hot-dog Skiing

Improved Categories
1. Competitive Sports
   A. Team Sports
   B. Individual Sports

In addition, categories should be fairly well balanced.

Unbalanced Categories
I. Reasons teenagers run away from home
   A. Alcoholic parents
   B. Rivalry with siblings
   C. Couldn't use the car
   D. Wanted a new dress
   E. Wanted to watch television
   F. Failed English

Improved Categories
I. Reasons teenagers run away from home
   A. Rivalry with siblings
   B. Quarrels with parents
   C. Problems at school

However, once the divisions are established, you can, almost without exception, arrange the entries in climactic order—from least important to most important—leaving the reader with the most significant point firmly imbedded in his or her memory.

EXERCISE

Beginning with a topic sentence, write a paragraph of at least 125 words which divides one of the following subjects into categories:

An effective social worker should demonstrate _____ qualities
An effective poem should demonstrate _____ qualities
An effective movie should demonstrate _____ qualities
An effective religious leader should demonstrate _____ qualities
An effective police officer should demonstrate _____ qualities
An effective parent should demonstrate _____ qualities
An effective in-law should demonstrate _____ qualities
An effective hostess (host) should demonstrate _____ qualities
An effective painting should demonstrate _____ qualities
An effective photograph should demonstrate _____ qualities
An effective dance concert should demonstrate _____ qualities
An effective musical composition should demonstrate _____ qualities
An effective mime performer should demonstrate _____ qualities
An effective stage actor should demonstrate _____ qualities
An effective TV singer should demonstrate _____ qualities
An effective history book should demonstrate _____ qualities
An effective teacher should demonstrate _____ qualities
An effective housekeeper should demonstrate _____ qualities
An effective salesperson should demonstrate _____ qualities
An effective employer should demonstrate _____ qualities
An effective employee should demonstrate _____ qualities
An effective doctor should demonstrate _____ qualities
An effective news reporter should demonstrate _____ qualities
An effective magazine should demonstrate _____ qualities
An effective TV commercial should demonstrate _____ qualities
An effective charity campaign should demonstrate _____ qualities

EXERCISE

Beginning with a topic sentence, write a paragraph of at least 125 words which divides one of the following subjects into categories:

An effective social worker should demonstrate _____ qualities
An effective poem should demonstrate _____ qualities
An effective movie should demonstrate _____ qualities
An effective religious leader should demonstrate _____ qualities
An effective police officer should demonstrate _____ qualities
An effective parent should demonstrate _____ qualities
An effective in-law should demonstrate _____ qualities
An effective hostess (host) should demonstrate _____ qualities
An effective painting should demonstrate _____ qualities
An effective photograph should demonstrate _____ qualities
An effective dance concert should demonstrate _____ qualities
An effective musical composition should demonstrate _____ qualities
An effective mime performer should demonstrate _____ qualities
An effective stage actor should demonstrate _____ qualities
An effective TV singer should demonstrate _____ qualities
An effective history book should demonstrate _____ qualities
An effective teacher should demonstrate _____ qualities
An effective housekeeper should demonstrate _____ qualities
An effective salesperson should demonstrate _____ qualities
An effective employer should demonstrate _____ qualities
An effective employee should demonstrate _____ qualities
An effective doctor should demonstrate _____ qualities
An effective news reporter should demonstrate _____ qualities
An effective magazine should demonstrate _____ qualities
An effective TV commercial should demonstrate _____ qualities
An effective charity campaign should demonstrate _____ qualities

CHAPTER 11 DEFINITION

Serious problems of communication may occur when you set down abstract terms for readers of widely differing backgrounds from your own. The word *war*, for instance, might mean one very specific thing to you. But does it mean the same thing to your local Army recruiter? To the person who writes patriotic songs about the flag? To the senator who is coming up for re-election? To the young widow whose husband was killed in Vietnam? To the Yale professor writing a book about ancient Assyria? To the five-year-old playing with a plastic tank? To the President of the United States?

It may, therefore, be necessary to explain to a reader exactly what you mean by a particular word. Such a definition may occupy a sentence, a paragraph, a long essay, or even an entire book. Anything longer than a sentence or two is called an *extended definition* and is used primarily (1) to explain a difficult term with which the reader may not be familiar, or (2) to explain a term which different people may interpret in different ways.

Before developing a definition, you may find it helpful to refer to the dictionary in order to familiarize yourself with points which had not occurred to you. But in no way are you limited to what you read there. An extended definition represents a personal interpretation, and may even contradict the dictionary as long as the definition is clear and reasonable.

Of the six most common ways to develop an extended definition, three depend upon methods of development already considered in this book:

1. classification and differentiation
2. anecdote (Chapter 5)
3. illustration (Chapter 7)
4. comparison and contrast (Chapter 8)
5. history
6. exclusion

DEFINITION BY CLASSIFICATION AND DIFFERENTIATION

Most dictionary definitions begin by placing a word in a general class and then explaining how that word differs from other members of the same class:

The term	Its general class	How it is different
A buggy	is a light four-wheeled carriage	with a single seat and a transverse spring.
A flintlock	is a gunlock	in which a piece of flint striking against steel produces sparks which ignite the priming.
The Vatican	is the palace	of the popes in Rome.
Narcissism	means sexual excitement	through admiration of oneself.

You may extend this dictionary method of classification and differentiation to a long discussion. To use this method, either classify and differentiate in your own way, or expand the definition you find in the dictionary, as in paragraph 42:

42 From earliest infancy the normal child obtains extreme sensual pleasure from such activities as thumb sucking, touching, tasting, and smelling. At the age of four or five, the child's pleasures are directed to his or her own body, in a stage which Freud called narcissism, after the youth in Greek mythology who fell in love with his own reflection in a pool of water. Healthy individuals will pass through this stage of narcissism to latency and finally to heterosexuality. But *narcissistic persons* are those who through abnormal amounts of shame, modesty, disgust, sympathy, or morality, spend their entire lives on the four or five-year-old level, forever in love with themselves.

Even though you consult a dictionary before you start to write, don't bore the reader by saying so. To begin by saying "Before talking about narcissism, let us turn to the dictionary to see what it says" is to take the most obvious but not the best route. Start off with what *you* want to say and let the reader consult the dictionary as desired. (See also Beginnings That Fail to Begin, No. 4, p. 88.)

DEFINITION BY ANECDOTE

Paragraph 43 develops a definition by telling a story which illustrates the word in question:

43 Graciousness means never suffering another person to feel discomfort or humiliation. Consider, for example, the young wife of the new sociology instructor. Recently hired for his first teaching assignment, the instructor was preparing a final examination for his students when his department head told him that the same multiple choice examination would be administered to all the Sociology I students at the university. The instructor decided that it would be helpful to his teaching the following term if he discovered what the examination looked like, so on the scheduled day he showed up to take the examination with the students. But when the answer sheets were run through the grading machine, he was horrified to learn that two of his students had scored higher than he had. Despondently he drove home, trying to decide whether he should give up teaching or merely take a few additional classes. But when he recited his miserable tale to his bride, she smiled comfortingly. "Don't be silly. That just proves what a great teacher you are. You can teach more than you know."

Definition

You may define a word by showing through examples how its concept operates, as in paragraph |44| :

|44| **DEFINITION BY ILLUSTRATION**

> The essence of *parenthood* is scrubbing: grass stains from pant knees, popsicle juice from noses and chins, chewing gum from hair and pockets, and grime from elbows, necks, ears, and fingernails. But parenthood requires other kinds of service as well. It means driving a frantic little first-grader to school because she knows she is going to be late and then having her saunter home twenty minutes later because she has forgotten a 10¢ rubber spider for Show and Tell. It means being awakened at 11:30 P.M. by a six-year-old who has just remembered that he needs a rabbit costume for the program at 10 A.M. It means having a solemn eight-year-old report that he has just volunteered your services to replace the Cub Scout den mother who resigned on doctor's orders. Most of all, parenthood means putting aside the pictures of relaxed and perfect families in the magazines and rolling up your sleeves.

You may define a term by explaining how it is or is not like something else.

DEFINITION BY COMPARISON AND CONTRAST |45|

> Poetry differs from prose in that it talks to the reader in many ways at once and thus says more in fewer words. In the first place, poetry more actively involves the reader's ear. For beyond the rhythm and rhyme of conventional verse forms, poetry also appeals to the ear through such devices as cadence, assonance, alliteration, and onomatopoeia. In the second place, poetry appeals more directly to the reader's eye, not only by describing with precision the details of the objective world but by providing metaphorical comparisons which sharpen the reader's perception. Finally, poetry more successfully communicates the author's feelings than does the typical prose paragraph and thus the poet and the reader more consistently share a common emotional experience.

Sometimes the changes in meaning that a word has taken on over a period of time will provide the basis for an interesting definition:

DEFINITION BY HISTORY |46|

> The concept of *family life* has changed considerably over the years. In earliest times several generations lived together in clans, which consisted of all living descendants and their husbands or wives. These clans were almost totally self-sufficient, every member contributing in some way toward the survival of the group. The men hunted and fished for food or sometimes maintained flocks of sheep or goats. The women ground flour, baked bread, and roasted the meat which their men provided. Special members of the community were selected to make pottery, weave baskets, tan skins, and hone weapons. But with the development of greater varieties of food, clothing, and shelter, a single clan could no longer develop all the individual skills that the group required. Clans merged into larger societies and at the same time broke into smaller units consisting of married couples and their children. Later the Industrial Revolution brought about even more important changes in family life. New inventions brought shorter working hours for men and easier housekeeping routines for women. Today a productive family life suggests not the group's cooperative efforts of working together, but the pleasant and meaningful sharing of its leisure.

Occasionally you may define a word by showing what it is not, rather than what it is:

DEFINITION BY EXCLUSION

[47] The literary-historical method of examining the Bible does not seize upon some verse or larger passage of scripture to "prove" a preconceived notion held by a church or individual. In fact, the method does not begin with any preconceived notions at all except the sincere belief that truth is worth seeking. Nor does it ignore the total situation in which the scripture was written, including possible dates, possible authors, and the attitudes, practices, political difficulties, and religious interpretations of the peoples of the time. Although the literary-historical approach to the Bible is sometimes called "higher criticism," it is not "higher" in the sense of functioning without the contributions of the language and translation specialists, sometimes called "lower critics." And it is not "criticism" in the sense of attempting to belittle Jehovah or his chosen people.

One final word of advice about extended definitions of all kinds: Having settled on a special meaning for a term, you must maintain your definition throughout the composition, unless, of course, you clearly explain to the reader that you are substituting a new definition and why.

EXERCISE

Using one of the six methods explained in this chapter, write a paragraph of at least 125 words defining one of the following terms:

Creativity	Radicalism
Science	Status
Rebellion	Police brutality
Passive resistance	Curiosity
Loneliness	Anti-intellectualism
Courtesy	Aggression
Charm	Gourmet cooking
Ignorance	Self-confidence
Self-control	Permissiveness
Peace of mind	Phoniness
Tradition	Propaganda
Demagoguery	Alienation

CHAPTER 12   REASONING

    Business reports, newspaper editorials, magazine articles—these are among the many kinds of writing which try to solve the problems encountered in human experience: Can the shipment of lockers be ready for installation before September 1? Does the traffic over State Highway 179 justify the construction of a new freeway? Are ungraded schools meeting the expectations hoped for them? Can the city afford the raise that the firefighters are demanding? Can it afford the consequences of refusing the raise?

    Such questions call for opinions or judgments formulated by reasoning—a process within the mind. Reasoning should be based upon the best facts available, but the resulting opinions will differ from the facts because (1) facts come from sources outside the mind, and (2)

facts are more easily proved. To understand the difference between opinions and facts, study the chart below:

Opinion	Fact
The elementary school counseling program is too expensive.	The elementary school counseling program cost the local school board $127,932.16 last year.
Senator Jarrett doesn't believe in the First Amendment.	Senator Jarrett introduced a bill last week to prevent the showing of explicit sex films at outdoor movie theaters.
The Heritage Foundation is ineffectual.	The Heritage Foundation failed in its efforts to prevent the owners from tearing down the old church on Market Street.
Democracy suffered a serious setback in June of 1969.	In June of 1969 the Supreme Court ruled that the House of Representatives could not deny a seat to a duly elected Congressman.

Frequently you, too, will have to formulate judgments in essay examinations, term papers, or perhaps even in committee reports. Possibly you will follow one of four common patterns:

1. Question to answer
2. Problem to solution
3. Effect to cause
4. Cause to effect

REASONING FROM QUESTION TO ANSWER

The most obvious method of developing an opinion paragraph is to begin with a question, follow it with whatever facts are available, and then end with the opinion which the facts lead to. Paragraph 48 serves as illustration:

48

Question — What effects have the U.S. government's programs to stem increasing world population had upon the underdeveloped nations of the world?

Facts — According to United Nations figures, the world population reached 3½ billion in 1968, with an annual increase of two percent, or seventy million people a year. Of this increase about eighty-five percent occurred in nations where more than half the people go to bed hungry each night. Although the governments of some of these nations are co-operating with the United States and the United Nations in trying to get population information to the people, it is obvious that the funds spent so far have not produced the results hoped for by our

Opinion — Congress.

Some questions, however, will call for more than one conclusion or opinion. The following paragraph lists five judgments in response to the question. Notice, however, that within each opinion are embedded facts which a scientist could probably verify:

Reasoning

Question	In what ways does the spewing of exhaust gases into the atmosphere menace human society? First is the damage to buildings, clothing, and other physical property, estimated at nearly twenty billion dollars annually. Polluted air contains chemical elements which rot brick, crumble stone, and even eat holes in metal. But more directly, the poisoned air seems to increase the frequency of lung diseases such as bronchitis, cancer, and asthma. And during periods of temperature inversions when a layer of warm air rests above a layer of cooler air and prevents the pollution from escaping, toxic elements in the atmosphere have caused actual deaths. Even more terrifying, however, are the long-range changes in the planet which carbon dioxide is bringing about. As a result of air pollution in the last seventy years, the temperatures of the atmosphere and oceans are gradually increasing. When the carbon content of the atmosphere becomes doubled, the glaciers at the poles will begin to melt, causing the oceans to rise and thus to flood the cities along the seacoasts.
first opinion	
second opinion	
third opinion	
fourth opinion	
fifth opinion	

A similar method of development is to state a problem and then solve it. In paragraph 50, the student writer explains the process by which certain French anthropologists reasoned out their conclusion about Neanderthal people:

REASONING FROM PROBLEM TO SOLUTION

Problem	French anthropologists have discovered surprising information about the Neanderthal people who lived in caves of the Middle East some sixty thousand years ago. Working in a cave about 250 miles north of Baghdad, Iraq, the French found several Neanderthal skeletons, one of which was surrounded by small mounds of pollen from such plants as the hollyhock, grape hyacinth, bachelor's button, and an unidentified evergreen shrub. The scientists reasoned that someone had carefully laid a corpse on a bier of flowers and boughs, for the pollen grains could not have been carried into the cave and so arranged by wind or four-footed animals. The ancient Neanderthals were therefore fairly sensitive creatures who maintained a higher degree of civilization than was heretofore believed.
Solution	

Paragraph 51 illustrates a still more sophisticated kind of problem-to-solution reasoning because the opinions of the writer (or rather the scientific opinions which are being reported on) are not based upon facts which are demonstrable at the present time. The writer, however, realizes that the judgments in the paragraph are theoretical and qualifies what is said with such expressions as "may be" and "probably":

Since space explorations beyond our solar system would take centuries, it seems difficult to believe that people from Earth would want to commit their entire lifetimes as well as the lifetimes of their children, grandchildren, and even great-grandchildren to a journey on a space vehicle. Nevertheless, if our solar system is ever colonized, there may be men and women who will never have known the sun and skies of earth but will have spent their entire lives under the surface of a planet like Mars, where the atmosphere is extremely thin, dry, and hostile to higher forms of life. Such people may be quite willing to trade their dark underground homes for huge spaceships equipped to sustain thousands of people for several hundred years. On these ships there would probably be room for great herds of animals and parklike gardens of fresh fruits and vegetables growing in chemicals rather than soil.

REASONING FROM EFFECT TO CAUSE

Another method of developing an opinion paragraph is by explaining a causal relationship. After establishing some event, circumstance, or statistic, you may suggest the cause or causes as you have reasoned them. An illustration follows:

52

Effect

Causes

Household fires, which destroy millions of dollars worth of property each year, are generally caused by one of the following situations: Careless smokers drop ashes on their rugs, sofas, or chairs or fall asleep in bed. Children discover matches which have not been safely locked up. Clothes have been hung on indoor lines too near furnaces or heated irons have been left unattended. Wastebaskets have been set near stoves or caution has not been used in melting wax and heating grease. Trash, paint, and dirty rags have been stored in warm closets, under stairs, or in wooden garages. People have been careless about poor wiring, damaged appliances, and overloaded fuse boxes.

REASONING FROM CAUSE TO EFFECT

Obviously, the order of the effect/cause relationship is reversible. In the paragraph below the writer sets down the cause (as historians have reasoned it) of Boston's first traffic law:

53

Transition

Cause

Effect

Of all the curious streets and sidewalks in Boston, one of the most interesting is a stretch of road some seven feet wide and about a block long. Officially its name is Change Alley, but more residents know it by its nickname, "Damnation Alley," a term it acquired many years ago from the hotheaded wagon drivers who would encounter each other in the street head on. Tempers in Change Alley became so fiery that at last the members of city government counseled together and agreed upon the following: "When drivers shall meet in these narrow streets they shall flip a coin to see which shall back out." That was Boston's first traffic law.

But the more typical cause-to-effect paragraph is the one in which the writer lists what he or she personally believes to be causes and effects. In paragraph 54 the writer reasons out two separate causal relationships:

Reasoning

Causes

Effect

Causes

Effects

Today's high school students, who have learned how to think—not merely to memorize, are frustrated by an educational system which they feel is not preparing them realistically for the society of the future. They are not interested in the kind of education their parents received. Many of them are already better informed than their parents about current issues, and they are unwilling to listen to parental advice about the importance of college training. They see, instead, the problems in their own high school classrooms and want to bring about changes immediately. They want more open class discussions about such things as birth control and drug abuse. They want to become involved in community action projects instead of listening to dehumanized TV lectures. They want fewer rules about smoking, haircuts, and manner of dress, but they want those few rules strictly enforced. But when parents, teachers, and school administrators fail to help them make the necessary changes, the young people either raise their voices or cease to talk at all. Often they imitate the campus protests of older college students, sometimes going beyond sign carrying and sit-down demonstrations to such violence as burning, bombing, and fighting.

From the examples of reasoning paragraphs in this chapter, you have seen that opinions may come from your own thinking or from the thinking of other people. But in either event you are responsible to your readers and must provide them with the soundest opinions possible.

EXERCISE

Beginning with a topic sentence, write a paragraph of at least 125 words, developed by question to answer, problem to solution, effect to cause, or cause to effect, on one of the questions below:

Does transplanting human organs raise any moral issues?
Does cremation raise any moral issues?
Does cremation solve any social issues?
Can Americans overcome the high cost of dying? (Rising funeral costs)
Are political and scientific values of space exploration worth the cost?
Should the institution of the family be preserved?
What effects do pornography have on the institution of the family?
Should pornography be controlled?
Can pornography be controlled?
Should wire-tapping evidence be permitted in court?
What are the arguments in favor of the pass-fail system?
What are the arguments in favor of contracting for grades?
Should life support systems be withdrawn from patients suffering from terminal illnesses?
Should patients suffering from terminal illnesses be given the opportunities for fast, painless death?
Do flying saucers really exist?
Is chastity out of date?
How does government infringe upon liberty?
Is there life after death?
Are American churches keeping up with the times?

CHAPTER 13 COMBINATION OF METHODS

Not every paragraph will illustrate a single, straightforward method of development. In fact, probably half of the paragraphs you read will combine two or more of the nine methods discussed previously in this book. The possibilities of combination are endless, but two paragraphs will serve for illustration here:

Problem Definition Solution Illustration	For many years scientists and artists have wondered how to prolong the "twilight zone" of human consciousness. This is the brief period of five or ten minutes when a person lies in bed neither fully awake nor fully asleep yet capable of creative insights and special learning processes which are impossible at other times. Now with the aid of an electromyograph (EMG) and a new device called a Twilight Learner, people can be taught to maintain the twilight state almost indefinitely so that they can also assimilate special kinds of information. The Twilight Learner has been used to teach students foreign languages, to help obese patients reduce, to encourage chain smokers and alcoholics to give up their habits, and to cure neurotic patients of their anxieties.	55
Analogy Illustration	Across the stage of America's political history have trooped some fascinating casts of minor political parties: the anti-Masonic party, the Know-Nothings, Barn Burners, Soft Hunkers, Populists, Grangers, Bull-Moosers, Progressives (of either the LaFollette or the Henry Wallace varieties), Socialists, Communists, Vegetarians, Prohibitionists, Silver Shirts, and Minute Men. Although many of them are not around long enough for even a	56

Analogy	curtain call, they can, like John Wilkes Booth, be troublesome while they are on stage. Some of these minor parties have expressed what might be called the *Politics of Protest* in behalf of particular interest groups. As a case in point, one thinks of the Granger movement of the 1870s seeking to protect farmers from railroad and grain storage monopolies. But others have expressed the *Politics of Status* for the psychologically, politically, and socially deprived among our people.
Definition	
Illustration	
Definition	

After having consciously attempted all of the nine methods of paragraph development defined heretofore in this book, you should be able to write well-developed paragraphs without worrying about what methods you are employing. The important things to remember are to be as concrete as possible, to focus on the controlling idea within each topic sentence, and to provide necessary transitions between individual sentences.

EXERCISE

Selecting one of the topics below and beginning with a topic sentence, write a paragraph of at least 125 words. When finished, identify what method or methods you have used by labeling them in the margin of the paper.

God is (is not) dead
American education is obsolete (forward-looking)
Love is blind
Antismoking commercials are stupid (worthwhile, discriminatory)
The death penalty is sadistic (justifiable)
Growing old gracefully
Image making: a big business in America
Worthless advice
Little white lies
Parents should (should not) monitor television viewing
Private enterprise should (should not) take over the mail service
Weather has become our worst enemy

PART III

THE WHOLE COMPOSITION

CHAPTER 14 PLANNING IN ADVANCE

THE THESIS STATEMENT

Before writing a whole composition, *you must set down your plan,* for only by the most remarkable luck will you ever write a successful theme or other paper which you have failed to plan in advance. The simplest and best kind of plan you can make for a whole composition is a thesis statement, which functions within the paper almost exactly the same way a topic sentence functions within a paragraph.

The Paragraph	The Whole Composition
Develops a single, fairly simple idea.	Develops a single, more thoughtful idea.
May contain a *topic sentence,* which summarizes the idea of the paragraph.	May contain a *thesis,* which summarizes the idea of the whole composition.
Will usually state the topic sentence at the beginning of the paragraph as a guidepost for both the reader and the writer.	Will usually state the thesis at the beginning of the composition as a guidepost for both the reader and the writer.

In a hurry to get their writing assignments completed, however, students sometimes fail to distinguish between a subject and a thesis and therefore do not make an appropriate plan beforehand. A subject is a general category, but a *thesis is an idea, opinion, or conclusion about the subject.* The chart below points up the difference:

Subject	Improved Subject	Thesis Statement
The Continental Congress	Problems facing the Continental Congress	The most important problem to be decided by the Continental Congress was whether or not the very idea of independence was desirable.
Cowboys	Black cowboys	American fiction and history books have over-

Planning in Advance

		looked the importance of blacks in the saga of the Chisholm Trail.
The national budget	Military appropriations in the national budget	The United States Congress must alter its priorities in appropriating money for defense.

A thesis statement, therefore, narrows the subject and contains an idea or opinion about it. But other qualities as well are necessary for a good thesis, as indicated by the paired examples below:

A. Can humans and grizzly bears live together in our national wilderness parks?
   (Poor thesis statement. No opinion, merely a question.)
B. If grizzly bears are to be protected, they should be given other habitats than national wilderness parks.
   (Improved thesis statement. Complete sentence contains an opinion or conclusion.)

A. A salesperson must be neat and clean so as to reflect your attitude.
   (Poor thesis. Not clearly expressed.)
B. A salesperson must be neat and clean to make a good impression on a prospective customer.
   (Improved thesis. Clear.)

A. The Bible is read by many people.
   (Poor thesis. Too vague.)
B. The Bible provides historical and geographical assistance to archeologists working in the region of the Fertile Crescent.
   (Improved thesis statement. More specific.)

A. Good nutrition is important.
   (Poor thesis. Too obvious.)
B. Poor nutrition caused serious dental problems for the Indians of Mesa Verde.
   (Improved thesis. Less widely known.)

A. Mexican food is revolting.
   (Poor thesis. Too emotional.)
B. Mexicans prepare highly seasoned dishes which some Americans find indigestible.
   (Improved thesis. Can be defended by reason.)

From the above material you will see that a good thesis statement

1. is best expressed in a complete sentence (never a question),
2. is clear,
3. focuses on a narrow aspect of the topic,
4. sets forth the writer's point of view,
5. is not an obvious opinion which every reader already shares,
6. can be defended by reason rather than emotion,
7. sets the pattern for the paper to follow.

Although professional writers will have their theses clearly in mind, they may not set them down on paper before they begin to write. But as a beginner, you should do more than merely think about what you plan to say. You should write a well-worded thesis statement on a piece of scratch paper before undertaking the introductory paragraph of a composition. Then repeat it as the first sentence of the paper or elsewhere in the introduction. (See pp. 85–86.)

Failure to plan a paper by writing a thesis statement in advance may result in one of three problems:

1. A paper which never contains any thesis but rambles on and on, saying nothing.
2. A paper which contains an accidental thesis but no evidence to support it.
3. A paper which contains two or more accidental theses which state widely separated, or even contradictory, opinions.

1. The student composition below illustrates the meandering and pointless kind of composition which occurs when the writer does not have a well-expressed thesis clearly in mind before beginning.

A Happy Experience

|57|

At the age of nineteen I was called to serve as an unpaid missionary for my church to the people of Samoa. I had never been all that enthusiastic about going on a mission, but I knew my parents had wanted me to go ever since I was a little child. My parents are wonderful people, and they have taught me so many good things of life that I don't believe that I can ever repay them enough for all they have done.

Religion, in my judgment, was for someone else. It was for older people about to die or other people who need comfort. I had my car, my job, my friends, my family, and everything I needed. And besides that, I wasn't sure the Bible was true. I had never read the Bible, and I had many doubts about the things I had heard in Sunday School. But after thinking things over, I decided a mission might be a way to better myself. I wondered if there was a purpose to life and if telling people about the gospel would bring joy and happiness to myself and others.

As I taught the Samoan people about this way of life, some could accept it while others were too set in their ways to change. I learned that religion was hard to teach to older people because they would usually say, "It is too late to change." But one old lady asked me to take charge of her husband's funeral, by saying a prayer and giving a sermon. It really touched my heart to make arrangements for the events of the next few days.

What a joy it is to know that death is not the end and that if you live righteously you will see your loved ones in heaven once again. When I came home from my mission, that old lady wrote me a letter saying she had decided to join the church. That was the happiest day of my life. I still have that letter and get it out to read whenever I feel lonely or discouraged.

How did the student's failure to compose a thesis lead him into difficulty? Are there any contradictions in the paper? Formulate a possible thesis for the composition. Then decide what supporting evidence the writer should strengthen or eliminate.

2. The next student composition contains an accidental thesis statement which the writer is unaware of and therefore fails to provide evidence for.

Planning in Advance 79

Problems of Heart Patients

Heart attacks may be accompanied by no pain or by minor pain in any part of the body. Thus, symptoms may fail to appear or may disguise themselves as other less frightening diseases. Often an attack will masquerade as indigestion or muscle cramps, for pain can come from the stomach, arms, legs, back, or head. And after an attack the symptoms may disappear quickly, never recurring in exactly the same way or part of the body. As a result, these "silent" heart attacks may go undetected for years. The victim may climb stairs, engage in heavy physical labor, or participate in active sports with no pain or shortness of breath.

Victims of undiscovered heart attacks face a greater risk of death than do patients who have formerly been hospitalized with a serious coronary. Discovering victims of these "silent" attacks is relatively simple if everyone—men, women, and children—will submit to a complete physical examination once a year. All that is necessary is a painless test in the office of the family physician. The doctor will ask the patient to perform some mild exercise—such as touching his toes several times or jogging in place for a brief period. Then the doctor will take a simple electrical recording of the heart on an EKG. Wires are attached to the patient's chest and limbs as the patient lies on a table. Pens on the machine mark a strip of moving graph paper, which the doctor then studies.

The resulting marks on the paper report how the heart is functioning and indicate whether or not there has been any previous damage from atherosclerosis. This disease gradually narrows and roughens the lining of the blood vessels until one or more vessels is completely blocked, sometimes through the additional presence of a clot. The part of the body served by that artery then cannot function from lack of fuel. If the blocked area is a major one, the patient will suffer serious pain and shock, but if the blocked area is a minor one, the symptoms may go unnoticed.

What is the accidental thesis in theme 58 above? How can the reader tell that the writer was not conscious of what was being said? How should the writer have organized the paper?

3. Illustration 59 below contains no overriding thesis, other than the student's emotional heat. Consequently, the writer sets down several accidental theses which contradict each other.

Higher or Lower?

The way higher education is being run these days is really disgraceful. Absolutely the worst part about American universities is the stupid, boring, sleep inducing, intellectually insulting "introductory" courses which every freshman is forced to sit through. A serious-minded student, planning to become a dentist, must fight yawns for a whole semester while some doddering old biologist describes the food preferences of mollusks. A talented young student, eager to pursue a career as a professional dancer, must memorize long, meaningless lists of chemical formulas. And whole classrooms full of future doctors, lawyers, stockbrokers, secretaries, salespersons, and scientists must fidget quietly while some stammering assistant professor takes four and one half months to define a "more" or a "primary group."

And the tests they give at universities! Nothing could be worse! All they test is the student's ability to write fast, spewing back some rote information from the textbook or class lectures. The poorly coordinated student, who cannot write quickly, might as well decide right now that he or she will never get A's in college. And the thoughtful student, who likes to collect all the necessary ideas before starting to write, is at a disadvantage, too. Speed, not originality or depth, is all that matters.

Even more unfair to students is the "publish or perish" policy for teachers, which keeps them from really teaching. In order to keep writing the required journal articles and textbooks, all the professors bury themselves in some remote library corner. They never stay in their offices to answer questions or make suggestions to students. And just ask some ghoulish secretary where Professor So-and-So is today. Those holier-than-thou secretaries they dig up to run the academic offices are definitely the most obnoxious characters in the whole university system.

But some of the teachers are even more maddening. First there are those beyond-retirement-age duffers who haven't read a new textbook or entertained a new idea in twenty years. Time has passed them by, and they don't even have the sense to know it. But nothing could be worse than those fresh young T.A.s who don't know a thing so they pretend to have invented science.

Yes, the whole university system is a pain in the neck.

Identify the contradictions in paper 59 above. Then consider possible ways of reorganizing the material by following the steps listed below:

1. Formulate a thesis which summarizes all the student's grievances but which is less emotional than the first and last sentences of the paper.
2. Compose an appropriate topic sentence for each of the supporting paragraphs.
3. Eliminate or provide evidence for any general statements which the student has failed to support.
4. Arrange the grievances in ascending or climactic order so that the most important one appears last for the reader to remember.

The following diagram will serve as a guide. It does not provide topic sentences for each paragraph, but it does suggest a possible overriding thesis and a possible arrangement for the supporting paragraphs. Notice that the material has been rearranged in climactic order.

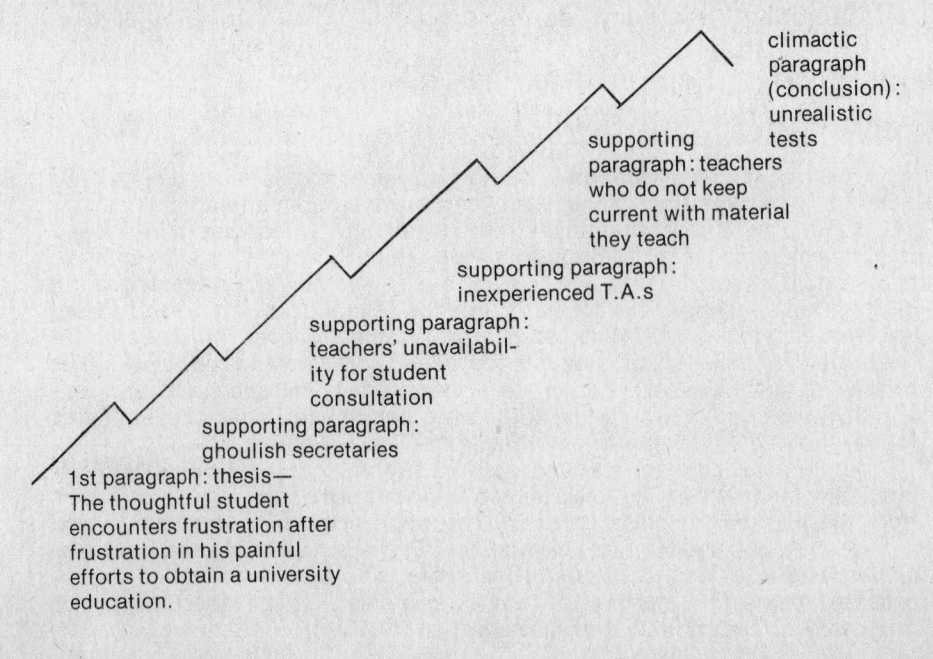

climactic paragraph (conclusion): unrealistic tests

supporting paragraph: teachers who do not keep current with material they teach

supporting paragraph: inexperienced T.A.s

supporting paragraph: teachers' unavailability for student consultation

supporting paragraph: ghoulish secretaries

1st paragraph: thesis—The thoughtful student encounters frustration after frustration in his painful efforts to obtain a university education.

Planning in Advance

The diagram shows how the concept expressed in the thesis statement can be divided into material for subsequent paragraphs.

Another way of breaking the thesis statement into elements is an informal outline which you will find helpful to jot down on a piece of scratch paper before you begin writing the paper. It will consist of the following:

INFORMAL OUTLINE

1. A well-worded thesis statement which you will probably re-state in the introductory paragraph.
2. Three to five sentences which support the concept expressed in the thesis and which you can expand into three to five paragraphs of approximately 150 words each.

Below are examples of three informal outlines:

Thesis: Developing communication with your husband (or wife) requires hard work.

1. You must plan a "talking time" every day.
2. You must pay attention to everything he (she) says.
3. You must shoulder your responsibility in conversation and be as witty and charming as you would like him (her) to be.
4. You must force yourself to be interested in the things he (she) truly enjoys.
5. You must sense his (her) psychological needs and make an effort to cater to them. (Climax)

Thesis: Adults force children to compete before they are psychologically ready to do so.

1. Games at children's birthday parties are too competitive.
2. Little League contests emphasize winning rather than sportsmanship and pleasure.
3. Younger and younger children are competing in Olympic games and other international events.
4. Wherever children are urged to win, one sees tears and unhappiness. (Climax)

Thesis: A patient's aim should be to handle stress, not to avoid it.

1. Diseases caused by stress have become the most important health problem in recent years.
2. Physical symptoms often indicate a patient's subconscious response to stress.
3. Periods of crisis and stress are necessary for personal growth.
4. Patients can learn about their inappropriate responses by going through psychotherapy.
5. A patient's control of internal states through electronic biofeedback devices is a newer and faster way to remove some symptoms of stress. (Climax)

Whenever possible, try to list the supporting elements of the informal outline in ascending or climactic order, since a strong point, stated last, relieves the burden of composing a more formal (and more difficult) conclusion for a paper.

EXERCISE A

Using one of the informal outlines on p. 81 write a theme of 400–600 words. Make certain that all paragraphs develop their topic sentences and support the overall thesis. Perhaps a change in the wording of the sentences in the outline may be necessary.

EXERCISE B

Composing your own thesis statement and informal outline in advance, write a theme of 400–600 words on one of the topics below:

An exploration
A scientific discovery
Gangster control of American businesses or political leaders
Gambling as a hobby or profession
Bribery in professional sports
Airplane accidents
Hijacking of airplanes
Dangers to or from hitchhikers
The future of education, democracy, medicine, or religion
Spiritualism: the art of communicating with the dead
Violence in America
Violence on television
American intervention in the politics of foreign nations
The monarchy in Great Britain
The Kennedys: an American dynasty
Beauty contests
Employing the physically or culturally handicapped
Changing roles of men and women in our society
The search for identity

CHAPTER 15   SOLVING PROBLEMS WHILE WRITING

Once the informal outline is on paper, the worry about translating rough notes into a finished paper disappears; for a good informal outline will provide such a clear plan that the only things left unsolved will be the beginning of the paper, the ending, and the transitions between paragraphs.

BEGINNINGS

By definition, an introduction should *introduce* a composition—both its subject matter and its tone—by indicating what is to follow. Unlike the supporting paragraphs in an expository paper, the introductory paragraph will probably be short. In fact, a long introduction is often a symptom of bad organization, suggesting that the writer (1) has not planned where the paper is headed or (2) does not know the difference between summary material and supporting material. Because a thesis statement is a summary of the whole paper, expressed as well as possible, it is usually the easiest and most direct beginning for a composition.

GOOD INTRODUCTIONS: THESIS BEGINNINGS

1. The first-sentence thesis. A good thesis will always make a good first sentence for a paper. It indicates the direction of the composition without talking down to the reader or sounding self-conscious. (See Poor Introductions, No. 6, p. 89.) Furthermore, by placing the thesis statement at the beginning, you will remind yourself what you are attempting to accomplish in the paper so that you will be on guard against irrelevant or contradictory comments.

Although the following thesis statements are short, they are long enough to serve as entire introductory paragraphs.

> Despite his successes, Lyndon Johnson will probably be remembered as the inventor of the "credibility gap."

> For every patriot who met at Philadelphia in 1776 to pledge "life, fortune, and sacred honor" to the cause of independence, there was a sober and successful Tory who saw treason in the act and disaster in the consequences.
>
> Having perfect pitch can be a serious disadvantage to a musical performer.

By breaking the thesis into two or three elements, you can indicate the design of the paper even more clearly.

> Sun Valley's highly successful tennis school operates under the theory that students should be taught court etiquette and form as well as game strategy.
>
> Marrying a lawyer means living with someone who expects to defend as a matter or principle an opinion that is wrong, to collect even when a case is lost, and to schedule all quarrels at least twenty-four hours in advance.

2. A question which leads directly to the thesis. A question often attracts the eye more quickly than a declaration and therefore may be a successful introduction to a piece of exposition. Because the beginning writer is apt to ask empty questions (See Poor Introductions, No. 5, p. 89), limit the question to one which is answerable in the next sentence by the thesis statement.

> What has nuclear weaponry done to the concept of war? It has eliminated "thinking time," or the luxury of mobilization.
>
> How do you train someone for football? Give ballet lessons, says one famous coach.

3. A contrast which emphasizes the thesis. The underlying idea of a paper may be heightened by contrasting it with circumstances of another time or situation.

> Fifty years ago, when airplanes were scarce and slow, pilots could anticipate trouble merely by watching the skies. Today, in the era of 600-mile-an-hour jets, the human eye is obsolete.
>
> Once the scene of solemn organ music, dignified masses, and thoughtful sermons, today's "relevant" church is trying to meet the needs of people by experimenting with such radical departures as contemporary music, masses served by clergymen in sports clothes, and the reading aloud of existential literature and world news events.

GOOD INTRODUCTIONS: DELAYED THESES (FOR ADVANCED STUDENT WRITERS)

No doubt the time will come when the three thesis beginnings listed above will no longer provide a challenge, and you will want to try other possibilities. Of course you realize already that good exposition can begin in a wide variety of ways. But any introduction which delays the thesis beyond the first paragraph poses risks for the inexperienced writer because the obvious sign-post is lost which keeps the writer on course, and he or she may eventually accidentally insert a second thesis which widens the focus of the paper or contradicts the underlying idea. Therefore, if you want to experiment with one of the additional good introductions below, you should still try to state the thesis within the first or second paragraph.

Solving Problems While Writing

4. A statement designed to startle the reader. A sentence which surprises the reader with frank or unusual information can often attract attention for the ensuing thesis.

> A golf club is more dangerous than a rifle. Although the freakish gun accident attracts newspaper headlines, quiet-living people who occasionally play a vigorous round of golf run a greater risk from heart attack than hunters do from injury by the stray bullets of their companions.
>
> Frightened New England ladies hid their Bibles when Jefferson was elected President. Rumors of Jefferson's Deistic philosophy, as evidenced by his fight for the separation of church and state, so alarmed many women of 1800 that they were certain he intended to deprive them of all forms of Christian worship.
>
> Patrick Henry boycotted the American Constitution. Henry, whose "liberty or death" speech has symbolized the faith and courage of America for two hundred years, refused to participate in the Constitutional Convention of 1787 because, he said, he "smelled a rat."

Sometimes the writer will startle the reader by deliberately misquoting a famous saying or creating some sort of pun.

> Douglas MacArthur is "The Unknown Soldier."
>
> Diapers are a girl's best friend.

5. A brief dramatic incident. A brief incident or story may provide a dramatic beginning for a paper. But in writing exposition you should remember that the main purpose is to explain an idea, not to tell a story. Therefore, be cautious about making the introductory narrative too long.

> A long limousine drove up to the British Embassy, and out wriggled a sleak black seal.
>
> "If you move a muscle, I'll blow your brains out," whispered a voice, hot on the back of my neck.
>
> In late September of 1862, a tall, unsmiling stranger walked past the city's Wells Fargo office on North C Street and into the two-story frame building next door.

6. A statement which relates the subject to a topic of current interest. Even a topic of limited historical interest can be meaningful if related to a topic of more immediate concern.

> During those late troubled years before his retirement in 1969, Earl Warren may have taken comfort in the realization that another famous jurist, Chief Justice Roger Taney, was once hanged in effigy.
>
> Those Americans worried about recurring predictions from astrologers, quasi-scientists, and Bible fundamentalists that the end of the world is at hand may be interested to know that the disaster is already 600 years behind schedule. The forthcoming Day of Judgment was confidently proclaimed in the *Nuremberg Chronicle* of 1493, an impressive five-pound volume published in Germany just as Columbus' sailors were returning home from their adventures in the New World.

7. A statement which anticipates the reader's possible objections. Argumentative writing may call for a comment which disarms possible critics.

> Although critics have denounced Thomas Paine's *Age of Reason* as both outdated and irresponsible, it makes several judgments which have been upheld by modern scholars.

8. A quotation. Worried about producing an original introduction, you can always borrow a striking quotation from someone else, preferably a recognized authority. Credit, of course, must be given.

> "If a leisured population is to be happy," advises Bertrand Russell, "it must be an educated population."
>
> Contrary to the view of modern psychologists, Machiavelli once said, "It is much more secure to be feared than to be loved."

These eight suggestions for good introductions are only a start. You will discover many more as you gain confidence and experience. But practicing with these few should keep anyone too busy to resort to the tedious openers listed below.

POOR INTRODUCTIONS: BEGINNINGS THAT FAIL TO BEGIN

1. The apology.

> Not being a music major, I don't know very much about . . . .
> I'm not sure if Hitler or Franco . . . .
> I wanted to write a paper on immunization in the nineteenth century but . . . .

2. The sentence which echoes the title or depends upon the title to be understood.

> **Problems of Television Programming**
> The problems of television programming are . . . .
>
> **Literary Criticism**
> This is a term which . . . .

Both problems of number 2 above are avoidable by delaying the composition of a title until the theme is completed. Furthermore, an appropriate title is easier to write after the paper is finished.

3. The dictionary definition. (Not to be confused with the extended definition discussed in Chapter 11.)

> Before talking about *imperialism,* let us turn to the dictionary to see . . . .
>
> According to Webster, *empathy* means . . . .

4. The inflated declaration of a commonplace or obvious idea.

> Philosophers have debated for centuries whether man is good or evil, and the argument certainly will never . . . .
>
> Food is necessary for the survival of every living . . . .
>
> Ever since the beginning of history people have engaged in wars . . . .

Solving Problems While Writing 89

5. **The meaningless question for which there is no answer.**

> What little boy or girl has never said he or she hated school . . . .
>
> What elderly person has failed to reflect . . . .

6. **The uninteresting announcement of the paper's intent.**

> In this paper I shall endeavor to prove . . . .
>
> There are three questions which I shall deal with . . . .

NOTE: A paragraph which sets forth the organization of the whole composition is called a partition paragraph. Although useful in a long or technical paper, a partition paragraph is seldom interesting enough to serve as the first paragraph of a composition. Instead, it should be placed immediately after the introduction in a paper where its use is justifiable.

In general, writing comes off much better if you don't struggle to begin with something profound or clever but merely *begin.* Don't be like the overzealous student who strains to convert a dull, empty idea into something unusual while burying a straightforward and well-expressed thesis in the second paragraph—or beyond. Just begin with the thesis itself if efforts to write a first paragraph are causing anxiety.

Another reason for difficulty may be that you are wrestling with a subject in which you simply are not interested. Certainly you will never entice someone else to read a paper which bores *you.* If necessary, ask the teacher for an alternative assignment rather than suffer with each word that you commit to paper.

ENDINGS

Contrary to what you may have always believed, *not every piece of exposition calls for a formal conclusion.* A *good* conclusion is always appropriate, of course. However, a short, simple theme with no formal ending will not seem to halt abruptly if (1) you have fully developed the thesis and (2) you have been careful to arrange the supporting paragraphs in climactic order with the most important detail or idea last. The kind of ending which merely repeats the beginning or summarizes the whole is very useful in a long or technical paper. But for most short English themes, such a conclusion is about as exciting as a dozen color television sets turned to the same channel. Unless you are trying to put the teacher to sleep, you should avoid the typical student paper with the obvious beginning, middle, and end, which read in essence: "In this paper I am going to prove three points . . . . I am now proving three points . . . . I have just proved three points . . . . "

But despite what has been said here, you may still feel uneasy about writing a paper with no formal conclusion. If so, your labor will be profitable, for the experience gained in writing good endings for short themes will prepare you for longer and more difficult papers. The five endings below are appropriate for either a short or a long paper.

GOOD CONCLUSIONS

1. A significant quotation which supports the thesis.

With Thomas Jefferson we therefore take the pledge of "eternal hostility against every form of tyranny over the mind of man."

In the words of Voltaire: "The happiest of all lives is a busy solitude."

"The dictum that truth always triumphs over persecution is one of those pleasant falsehoods which men repeat one after another till they pass into commonplaces, but which all experience refutes." John Stuart Mill.

2. An anecdote, or story, which illustrates the thesis.

Too many Americans are more concerned with what their neighbors think than with what they themselves believe. They are like the fearful man who wouldn't enroll in the college evening class until he had checked out all the other students to make certain there were no communists, dissidents, or other undesirables among them. "My wife and I," he explained, "never join any group which might expose us to suspicion or gossip."

Obviously, a Pollyanna-ish optimism will not solve every crisis. I am reminded, for instance, of the old lady who dressed up each morning for the visitors she hoped would call. But she was so busy staying home waiting for company that she never had time to go out and make friends.

3. A solution for a problem presented in the composition.

Because the pass-fail system has not worked does not mean that we should return to the old emphasis on academic grades and mathematical GPAs. An individualized and less rigid evaluation system than letter grades is necessary. Perhaps some modification of the method used in the early grades—where teachers write brief comments about each student—would be the best alternative.

Countries, like parents, may find that greater cooperation comes from fewer challenges to the sense of importance and self-esteem.

4. A statement designed to make the reader think about or act upon the problem suggested by the paper.

Yet it is not more than five hundred years since the great empire of the Aztecs still believed that it could live only by the shedding of blood. Every year in Mexico hundreds of human victims died in this fashion: the body was bent like a bow over the curved stone of sacrifice, the breast was slashed open with a knife of obsidian, and the priest tore out the beating heart of the still living victim. The day may be close at hand when we shall no longer tear out the hearts of men, even for the sake of our national gods. Let the reader refer to the earlier time charts we have given in this history, and he will see the true measure and transitoriness of all the conflicts, deprivations, and miseries of this present period of painful and yet hopeful change.

H.G. Wells, *The Outline of History**

---

* H.G. Wells, *The Outline of History,* (New York: Macmillan Company, 1921).

> If a man cares enough about his wife to reduce the years she must spend in lonely isolation as a widow, he will pay closer attention to his eating habits and physical activities.

5. A memorable restatement of the thesis through the use of figures of speech, emphasis, balance, or other qualities of distinguished prose.

> I do not say that John or Jonathan will realize all this, but such is the character of that morrow which mere lapse of time can never make to dawn. The light which puts out our eyes is darkness to us. Only that day dawns to which we are awake. There is more day to dawn. The sun is but a morning star.
>
> Henry D. Thoreau, *Walden*

> With such demonstrations of affection for our Constitution; with an adequate organization of the militia; with the establishment of necessary fortifications; with a continuance of those judicious and spirited exertions which have brought victory to our Western army; with a due attention to public credit, and an unsullied honor toward all nations, we may meet, under every assurance of success, our enemies from within and from without.
>
> George Washington, "Address to the Senate"
> November 22, 1794

Or for a long paper you may use the more familiar ending:

6. A summary of the major points in the composition.

> Therefore, a small car has the advantages of economy and maneuverability but is not always the better investment. The considerations of death or permanent injury to occupants of a small car are often more important.

Try to avoid the common but ineffective conclusions listed below:

1. the conclusion which introduces new information or new problems not covered in the paper itself, and
2. the conclusion which shifts to a tone of exhortation, or preaching.

POOR CONCLUSIONS

TRANSITIONS BETWEEN PARAGRAPHS

Like the individual paragraphs within it, an entire composition must cohere, or "stick" together. In addition to the transitional devices discussed in Chapter 2, the techniques below may be useful within a longer composition.

1. Use of short transitional paragraphs.
2. Use of a final sentence in a paragraph which suggests the next topic idea.
3. Use of a beginning sentence in a paragraph which refers to the final sentence or topic idea of the preceding paragraph. Since for the time being you are trying to place a topic (summary) sentence at the beginning of each paragraph, you may move the topic sentence to the second position when you begin the paragraph with a transition.
4. Use of a sustained comparison or figure of speech.

The paper below illustrates how all four of these techniques may operate within a single short composition.

Unmasking the University

60 A good deal of masquerading takes place in the world of higher education. Many hundreds of institutions across this land—with benefit of clergy, legislature, trustees, and/or alumni—call themselves universities. But the fact is that many of them are mere classrooms attached to football teams, Greek letter societies, debate clubs, dance recitals, little theater presentations, or cheap political and religious doctrines.

What then is a University?

At the core it must have a certain attitude toward knowledge, a sincere humility in regard to truth, before a university is really worthy of the name. There are some institutions of higher learning so committed to a particular church, philosophy, or doctrine that they comfortably assume they possess all Truth. Certainly in a free society there is room and need for such institutions. But they are not universities. A university neither possesses nor dispenses Truth. Instead, it offers to students many possible truths and encourages both faculty and students to press on in the search for all truth, wherever the quest may lead.

It might be a kind thing for a university to give entering freshmen a forewarning about the quest ahead. The sign at the entrance of Dante's Inferno could perhaps be placed at the registration table—"Abandon all hope, ye who enter here"—all hope of quick answers and ready formulas. In short, "Freshmen, take heed. Fondly-held beliefs, unexamined prejudices, values learned at mothers' knees are going to be tested, challenged, and possibly even fractured before the course is run."

Those students who need a seminary but find themselves at a university may expect to find Truth served up unconditionally in the classroom: Truth on evolution in Biology 101, Truth on inflation control in Economics 213, and Truth on Richard Nixon in Political Science 118. But they will discover that the conclusions so neatly reached in Biology 101 may be challenged in Biology 151. Or the convictions asserted in Political Science 118 and reaffirmed in Political Science 280 may be undermined in Political Science 345—or in the library—or in a bull session in the student dormitory. The locations of answers will vary for different students and quite possibly never be found at all. The only thing certain is that the quest will be wearisome for all who undertake it and painful for many.

Upon reaching a university, therefore, a student must comprehend quickly that the journey upon which he is embarking requires both effort and discomfort. The student must expect his values and pet beliefs to undergo some intellectual mauling along the way. Furthermore, he should realize as early as possible why such mauling is essential to the learning process.

For a true university—not simply a few buildings in the costume of a university—requires opposing viewpoints among faculty members, among authors of textbooks, even among the students themselves.

---

*J.D. Williams, "A University Education," *The Eleusis* (Chi Omega), 1959.

EXERCISE A

Write an introductory paragraph for a paper based on each of the three thesis statements below (a total of three separate introductions for three separate papers). Beside each one identify which method you have used from the list beginning on p. 85, Good Introductions: Thesis Beginnings.

1. Bragging proves people do (don't) like themselves.
2. Guilt is a useless emotion.
3. Dieters usually regain the weight they lost while dieting.

EXERCISE B

Write a concluding paragraph for a paper based on each of the two thesis statements below (a total of two separate conclusions for two separate papers). Beside each one identify which method you have used from the list beginning on p. 90, Good Conclusions.

1. Praise is often (seldom) a better reward than money.
2. Immaturity (sex, in-laws, money, religion) is the most common source of marital conflict.

EXERCISE C

Copy "Unmasking the University" from p. 92 on notebook or type paper, leaving wide margins and skipping every other line. Re-read Transitions Between Paragraphs before you begin.

1. Identify all short transitional paragraphs with red pen or pencil.
2. Identify all final sentences in paragraphs which suggest the next topic idea with green pen or pencil.
3. Identify all beginning sentences in paragraphs which refer to a final sentence or topic idea of preceding paragraph with black pen or pencil.
4. Identify sustained comparisons or figures of speech with yellow pen or pencil.

PART IV

FUNDAMENTALS OF ENGLISH PROSE

CHAPTER 16 GLOSSARY OF USAGE

What would you think if you were dining at an expensive hotel when the man at the next table suddenly whipped out a bottle of mouthwash, unscrewed the lid, and started gargling loudly? Maybe the irregularity of the situation and the noise wouldn't be too bothersome, but if he tried spitting the mouthwash into his water glass or into his soup bowl, would your discomfort increase? Well, how would you feel if he were to brush his teeth at the table? Would that bother you as much? Would you mind if he merely picked his teeth—with the cardboard from a book of matches, say? If he used a toothpick? If he tried to hide what he was doing behind a large napkin? Surely you will agree that all of these possible offenses are not equally annoying, but perhaps you would prefer him to take care of all his oral hygiene elsewhere—not at a fancy restaurant. Still, the man's actions might not bother you as much as those of the lady who put on foolish airs when you took her camping—the lady who tripped all over the platform shoes she wore hiking.

Yes, good manners are largely a matter of time and place. Some actions are always in good taste. But other actions, perfectly reasonable and healthful in certain situations, become inappropriate and even disgusting if undertaken at the wrong time. And not all offensive actions are equally offensive.

The same thing is true of the words people use. Some words are never out of place, but others are too lowbrow (or occasionally too highbrow) to be used except in very limited situations. English instructors often refer to these degrees of respectability as four main levels of usage—(1) illiterate or substandard, (2) dialectal or colloquial, (3) formal or standard, and (4) very formal. Usually teachers encourage students to eliminate words and expressions from the two lowest levels from all their college writing.

Glossary of Usage

LEVELS OF ENGLISH USAGE

Dialectal (regional) and Colloquial (conversational) English

Use in writing:
   Diaries
   Letters to close friends
   Classroom notes
   Some newspaper sports and society columns
   Some articles in teen-age magazines, sports magazines, movie magazines

Formal (standard) English—always appropriate

Use in writing:
   English compositions
   College term papers
   Newspaper editorials
   Most magazine articles
   Business letters
   Job applications

Very formal English

Use in writing:
   Master's theses
   Doctoral dissertations
   Papers to be read to professional societies
   Articles in professional journals

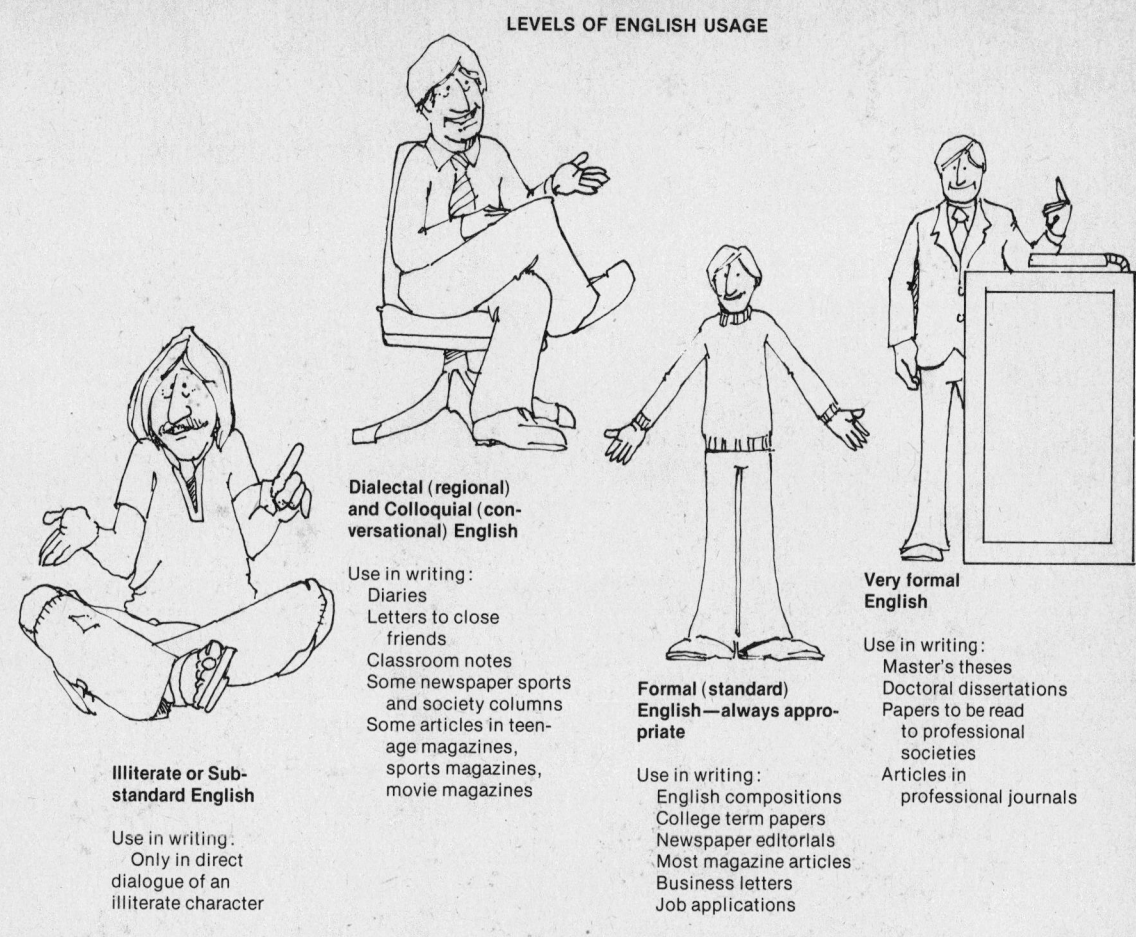

Illiterate or Sub-standard English

Use in writing:
   Only in direct dialogue of an illiterate character

Ad — *Advertisement* is preferable in formal writing.

Aggravate — The formal meaning of the word is "to make worse." Avoid using it as a synonym for "annoy" or "irritate."
   The dog's barking aggravated me. (Colloquial)
   The dog's barking irritated me. (Standard)
   The dog's barking aggravated my headache. (Standard)

Ain't — *Aren't, isn't,* and *am not* are the correct terms.
   I ain't coming. (Illiterate)
   I am not coming. (Standard)

All the farther, all the faster — *As far as* and *as fast as* are preferable.
   Chapter 10 was all the farther I did the assignment. (Colloquial)
   Chapter 10 was as far as I did the assignment. (Standard)
   Sixty miles an hour is all the faster my car will go. (Colloquial)
   Sixty miles an hour is as fast as my car will go. (Standard)

Almost — See **Most**.

Alright *All right* is the correct spelling.

Among, between *Among* usually refers to three or more. *Between* usually refers to only two.
   Mother divided the pie among the five of us. (Standard)
   Just between the two of us, I don't trust Andy. (Standard)

And, but, for, nor, or, so, yet These seven coordinating conjunctions were once considered inappropriate as the first words in written sentences. However, authorities now prefer them to the heavier transitional connectives (*therefore, consequently, moreover, indeed,* etc.) except in very formal writing.
   Therefore, the word was disseminated that one should not take a public stand on the Scopes trial. (Very formal)
   So the word was broadcast that a man should not take a public stand on the Scopes trial. (Standard)

And etc. The *and* is redundant. Because *etc.* (abbreviation for *et cetera*) means "and so forth," *and etc.* would mean "and and so forth."

Anyplace, anywheres *Anywhere* is preferable.
   She could not find her book anyplace. (Colloquial)
   She could not find her book anywheres. (Dialectal or illiterate)
   She could not find her book anywhere. (Standard)

Aren't This word is colloquial when used with the pronoun *I*.
   I am invited, aren't I? (Colloquial)
   I am invited, am I not? (Very formal)
In order to find a compromise between the colloquial and very formal constructions above, you may prefer to revise the entire sentence.

As Do not use for *whether* or *that*.
   I do not know as I can go. (Colloquial)
   I do not know whether I can go. (Standard)

As, as if, as though See **Like**.

At See **Where at**

At about *About* is preferable.
   I will call for you at about nine. (Colloquial)
   I will call for you about nine. (Standard)

Auto *Automobile* is preferable in formal writing.

Awful, awfully *Very, surely, certainly* are preferable as intensifiers.

Badly Do not use for "very much"; do not use after the verb "feel."
   I badly want to go to the Junior Prom. (Colloquial)

Glossary of Usage

I very much want to go to the Junior Prom. (Standard)
I feel badly. (Colloquial)
I feel bad. (Standard)

Balance Do not substitute for *the remainder, the rest, the others* (except in reference to a bank balance or mathematical problem).
The balance of the meal was delicious. (Colloquial)
The rest of the meal was delicious. (Standard)

Beautiful See **Cute.**

Because See **Reason is because.**

Being as, being that Do not substitute for *since* or *because.*
Being that Laurie was absent seven times, the teacher gave her a C. (Colloquial or illiterate)
Because Laurie was absent seven times, the teacher gave her a C. (Standard)

Beside, besides Do not use these two words interchangeably. *Beside* means "by the side of." *Besides* means "in addition to."
Come sit besides me. (Illiterate)
Come sit beside me. (Standard)
No one filed an application beside Dena. (Illiterate)
No one filed an application besides Dena. (Standard)

Blame on The *on* is inappropriate.
The coach blamed the defeat on Elswood. (Colloquial)
The coach blamed Elswood for the defeat. (Standard)

But what, but that Do not substitute these terms for *that.*
I have always been certain but what Kyle will graduate with honors. (Colloquial)
I have always been certain that Kyle will graduate with honors. (Standard)

Cannot help but This form is in dispute. A construction omitting either *not* or *but* is preferable.
I cannot help but hope for a raise. (Colloquial)
I cannot help hoping for a raise. (Standard)
I can but hope for a raise. (Very formal)

Center around *Center on* is preferable.
The executive committee discussion centered around the new sports complex. (Colloquial)
The executive committee discussion centered on the new sports complex. (Standard)

Character People have character. Things have characteristics, properties, or features.

The campus had an impressive character. (Colloquial)
The campus had impressive features. (Standard)

Complected

Complexioned is preferable.
The singer was light-complected. (Colloquial or dialectal)
The singer was light-complexioned. (Standard)

Could not hardly, could not scarcely

The two negative words (*not* and *hardly*) result in an ungrammatical double negative.
I could not hardly wish for a better geometry teacher. (Colloquial)
I could hardly wish for a better geometry teacher. (Standard)

Could of, would of, might of

Do not substitute for *could have, would have, might have.*

Critique

Use this word as a noun, not as a verb.
I critiqued *A Farewell to Arms* for my film history class. (Colloquial)
I wrote a critique on *A Farewell to Arms* for my film history class. (Standard)
I criticized *A Farewell to Arms* for my film history class. (Standard)

Cute, fine, nice, great, elegant, beautiful, swell, lovely, tremendous

Do not overwork these words as vague terms of approval. Use the exact word.

Died with

Died of is preferable.
Lawrence died with cancer. (Colloquial)
Lawrence died of cancer. (Standard)

Different than

Different from is preferable.
The history of Concord is different than the history of Salem in many ways. (Colloquial)
The history of Concord is different from the history of Salem in many ways. (Standard)

Dilemma

The word *dilemma* indicates a situation in which one faces two or more equally unpleasant alternatives. Do not use it as a synonym for *problem* or *trouble*.
I had a dilemma about which job to accept. (Colloquial unless you didn't like any of the job offers.)
I had a problem about which job to accept. (Standard)

Don't

This contraction for *do not* calls for a plural (never a singular) subject.
It don't matter to me. (Colloquial or illiterate)
It doesn't matter to me. (Standard)
They don't matter to me. (Standard)

Glossary of Usage

Elegant   See **Cute.**

Enthused   *Enthusiastic* is preferable.
>I was not enthused about the matinee. (Colloquial)
>I was not enthusiastic about the matinee. (Standard)

Equally as good   The *as* is redundant.
>Her chocolate cake was equally as good as mine. (Colloquial)
>Her chocolate cake was equally good as mine. (Standard)

Every place   *Everywhere* is preferable.

Exam   *Examination* is preferable in formal writing.

Expect   Do not substitute for *suppose* or *surmise.*
>I expect Glenna failed chemistry because she cheated on her laboratory experiments. (Colloquial)
>I suppose Glenna failed chemistry because she cheated on her laboratory experiments. (Standard)

Farther, further   In formal writing, *farther* usually refers only to distance and *further* only to time, quantity, or degree.
>We journeyed farther the first day. (Standard)
>After her illness, Jean further postponed her marriage. (Standard)

Fewer, less   *Fewer* refers to number (things which can be counted). *Less* refers to degree, value, or amount. Plural countable nouns will therefore take the adjective *fewer.*
>Fewer people drink less milk. (Standard)

Fine   See **Cute.**

Fun   This word is properly used as a noun, not an adjective or verb.
>I enjoy having fun. (Standard)
>We had a fun time. (Dialectal)
>The boys were funning around. (Dialectal)

Great   See **Cute.**

Gym   *Gymnasium* is preferable in formal writing.

Hadn't ought   Avoid this expression.
>I hadn't ought to have eaten so much. (Illiterate)
>I shouldn't have eaten so much. (Standard)

Have got   The *got* is redundant.
>I have got a farm near Madison. (Colloquial)
>I have a farm near Madison. (Standard)

Heighth   *Height* is preferable.

Hisself, theirselves	Do not use for *himself, themselves*. 　　Wally could not dress hisself after he broke his arm. (Illiterate) 　　Wally could not dress himself after he broke his arm. (Standard)
How come	*Why* is preferable. 　　How come Chemistry 115 is required for graduation? (Colloquial) 　　Why is Chemistry 115 required for graduation? (Standard)
Hung	*Hanged* is correct for an execution; *hung* is correct for inanimate objects. 　　The Salem courts hanged 21 witches in one year. (Standard) 　　The artist hung all his pictures in the new gallery. (Standard)
In the case of, in some cases, in this case, etc.	These expressions add unnecessary words to prose. Use them sparingly, if at all. 　　In the case of football, proper equipment can often prevent serious injury. (Colloquial and wordy) 　　Proper equipment can often prevent serious injury in football. (Improved)
Inside of	*Inside* or *within* is preferable. 　　The committee will meet inside of a week. (Colloquial) 　　The committee will meet within a week. (Standard)
Irregardless	*Regardless* is correct. 　　Janna is going to marry Jim irregardless of the consequences. (Colloquial or illiterate) 　　Janna is going to marry Jim, regardless of the consequences. (Standard)
Is when, is where	These terms are awkward in definition. 　　A sonnet is when 14 lines of iambic pentameter rhyme in a definite pattern. (Colloquial) 　　A sonnet is a 14-line iambic pentameter poem, rhyming in a definite pattern. (Standard)
Kind, sort	Because these words are singular, they should be modified by singular adjectives. 　　I like these kind of nuts. (Colloquial) 　　I like this kind of nuts. (Standard)
Kind of, sort of	Do not substitute for *somewhat, in some degree, almost, rather*. 　　The lecture seemed sort of long. (Colloquial) 　　The lecture seemed rather long. (Standard)
Knowledgeable	Although this term is gaining acceptance, many authorities still regard it as a colloquial substitute for *intelligent* or *well-informed*. The *-able* suffix denotes ability, liability, or tendency. Therefore, the logical meaning of the word would be someone capable of knowledge, not someone already possessing it.

Glossary of Usage

    A knowledgeable scientist spoke to us about radioactive fall-out. (Colloquial)
    A well-informed scientist spoke to us about radioactive fall-out. (Standard)

Lab *Laboratory* is preferable in formal writing.

Lend, loan In standard English, *lend* is a verb and *loan* is a noun.
    I will loan you $10. (Colloquial)
    I will lend you $10. (Standard)
    The loan was $10. (Standard)

Like Avoid using *like* as a conjunction. *As, as if,* and *as though* are preferable.
    Do like I say, not like I do. (Colloquial)
    Do as I say, not as I do. (Standard)
    He acted like he wanted to come. (Colloquial)
    He acted as if he wanted to come. (Standard)

Lose out, miss out, win out The *out* in these combinations is wordy and inappropriate.
    Virtue will win out in the end. (Colloquial)
    Virtue will win in the end. (Improved)
    Virtue will triumph in the end. (Better still)

Lots of, a lot of Do not substitute for *many* or *much.* Never spell *a lot* as one word.
    Alot of us misjudge people in public life. (Illiterate)
    A lot of us misjudge people in public life. (Colloquial)
    Many of us misjudge people in public life. (Standard)

Lovely See **Cute.**

Most Do not substitute for *almost.*
    We accept most all credit cards. (Colloquial)
    We accept almost all credit cards. (Standard)
    We accept most credit cards. (Standard)

Nice See **Cute.**

No place *Nowhere* is preferable.

Nowhere near Do not substitute for *not nearly.*
    Jill was nowhere near as tired as I was. (Colloquial)
    Jill was not nearly as tired as I was. (Standard)

Off of, out of The *of* is unnecessary.
    The cat climbed off of the piano and out of the window. (Colloquial)
    The cat climbed off the piano and out the window. (Standard)

Only Do not substitute for *but* or *except that.*
    I wanted to come, only it started to rain. (Colloquial)

I wanted to come, but it started to rain. (Standard)
I would have come except that it started to rain. (Standard)

Over with The *with* is unnecessary.
Now that test week is over with, can you go to California? (Colloquial)
Now that test week is over, can you go to California? (Standard)

Phone *Telephone* is preferable in formal writing.

Photo *Photograph* is preferable in formal writing.

Plan on going Do not substitute for *plan to go*.

Plus, plus the fact Do not use *plus* as a synonym for the conjunction *and*. Do not use *plus the fact* in place of the expression *in addition to the fact*.
I had steak, potatoes, plus green salad for dinner. (Colloquial)
I had steak, potatoes, and green salad for dinner. (Standard)
Jane's tact plus her zeal make her a valuable employee. (Colloquial)
Jane's tact plus zeal make her a valuable employee. (Colloquial)
Jane's tact and zeal make her a valuable employee. (Standard)
Plus the fact that he has used up all his sick leave, Jake has been late seven times. (Colloquial)
In addition to the fact that he has used up all his sick leave, Jake has been late seven times. (Standard)

Prejudice, use Do not substitute for *prejudiced, used*.
Collins is prejudice against foreigners. (Illiterate)
Collins is prejudiced against foreigners. (Standard)
I am use to a steak and three eggs for breakfast every morning. (Illiterate)
I am used to a steak and three eggs for breakfast every morning. (Standard)

Refer back

Glossary of Usage

Pretty near, pret' near
Do not substitute for *nearly* or *almost*.
It was pret' near nine o'clock before the bus arrived. (Dialectal)
It was pretty near nine o'clock before the bus arrived. (Colloquial)
It was nearly nine o'clock before the bus arrived. (Standard)

Put in for
Do not use for *apply* or *applied*.
I am going to put in for a job with the Xerox Corporation. (Colloquial)
I am going to apply for a job with the Xerox Corporation. (Standard)

Reason is because, reason is on account of
Reason is that is preferable.
The reason Ron will not be there is because he has to tend his little sister. (Colloquial)
The reason Ron will not be there is that he has to tend his little sister. (Standard)

Refer back
The *back* is unnecessary.
For additional explanation, refer back to page 20. (Colloquial)
For additional explanation, refer to page 20. (Standard)

Same, said, such
Do not use these words as pronouns except in legal documents. *It, this,* and *that* are preferable.
When I examined my car, I saw the same was dented on the left side. (Colloquial)
When I examined my car, I saw that it was dented on the left side. (Standard)

Show up
Appear or *be present* is preferable.
I hope Lewis will show up for the hearing. (Colloquial)
I hope Lewis will appear for the hearing. (Standard)

So, such
Do not use as intensifiers in formal writing.
I am so hungry. (Colloquial)
I am very hungry. (Standard)
These words are correct when followed by a clause introduced by *that*.
I am so hungry that I could eat my shoes. (Standard)

Some
Do not substitute for *somewhat, a little*.
We were some exhausted after the long hike. (Colloquial)
We were somewhat exhausted after the long hike. (Standard)

Some place, someplace
Somewhere is preferable.

Sure
Do not use as an adverb in place of *surely, certainly, very*.
Professor Rosenblatt sure gives difficult tests. (Colloquial)
Professor Rosenblatt surely gives difficult tests. (Standard)

Suspicion
Do not use as a verb meaning *suspect*.

I suspicioned the butler committed the murder with a candlestick. (Colloquial)
I suspected the butler committed the murder with a candlestick. (Standard)

Swell See **Cute.**

That there, this here These terms are illiterate for *that, this.*

Them Do not use as an adjective.
I want to buy one of them guns. (Illiterate)
I want to buy one of those guns. (Standard)

Tremendous See **Cute.**

Try and *Try to* is preferable.
Please try and finish the assignment by Monday. (Colloquial)
Please try to finish the assignment by Monday. (Standard)

Use See **Prejudice.**

Way Do not substitute for *condition.*
Jeremy was in a bad way on Sunday. (Colloquial)
Jeremy was in poor condition on Sunday. (Standard)

Ways Do not use this word as a substitute for *way* or *distance.*
We have a long ways to go before dark. (Colloquial)
We have a long way to go before dark. (Improved)
We have a long distance to go before dark. (More formal)

Where at The *at* is unnecessary.
Where did you buy the sweater at? (Colloquial. Considered illiterate by some authorities.)
Where did you buy the sweater? (Standard)

Without, without that Do not substitute for *unless.*
You must pay your fine promptly without you want to go to jail. (Colloquial or dialectal)
You must pay your fine promptly unless you want to go to jail. (Standard)

Would better *Had better* is the preferred expression.
You would better get your resignation to the secretary before Thursday. (Colloquial or illiterate)
You had better get your resignation to the secretary before Thursday. (Standard)

Would have Do not substitute for *had.*
If you would have driven more slowly, the accident might have been prevented. (Colloquial)
If you had driven more slowly, the accident might have been prevented. (Standard)

EXERCISE

Revise any words or phrases which are inappropriate for formal writing. If a sentence is correct, put C in the blank to the left. (Sentences may contain more than one error.)

_____ 1. If you would have turned in your assignment on time, the teacher might not be aggravated.

_____ 2. You would better get your application to the committee by Thursday without you want it put in the wastebasket.

_____ 3. Five hundred words a minute was all the faster I could read before I saw the newspaper ad about the speedreading course.

_____ 4. Where did you study Hebrew at?

_____ 5. I will try and let you know as soon as possible if your grades are really in a bad way or if the registrar is just prejudice.

_____ 6. Just between the two of us, I consider Banham's paper equally good as mine.

_____ 7. Today's children know less ways of having a fun time than the children of twenty-five years ago.

_____ 8. I am different from Jan, aren't I?

_____ 9. I cannot help but feel badly that you could not find the check anyplace.

_____ 10. He sounded like he was awful uncertain, but he said he would be there at about 5:30 P.M.

_____ 11. The reason I got the only *A* is because the balance of the class misunderstood the assignment.

_____ 12. Being as the discussion centered around boxing, I could not hardly ask my question about Mickey Mantle.

_____ 13. The interior decorator blamed the shabby character of the room on the old blue sofa.

_____ 14. I have always been certain but what Gene died with self-induced poisoning.

_____ 15. Irregardless of your opinion, I like this kind of nuts.

_____ 16. Dr. King's lab technician is knowledgeable about most all acids and lots of explosives.

_____ 17. Now that test week is over with, do you plan on going someplace for a short vacation?

_____ 18. It was pretty near the deadline before I put in for a scholarship.

_____ 19. She was use to going without a sweater, only she did not expect snow.

_____ 20. Dena was nowhere near as sick as Pete, but they both acted like they were going to die.

_____ 21. How come you have got fourteen misspelled words?

_____ 22. Gail is sort of light complected.

_____ 23. I am not enthused about taking the Ph.D. exam.

_____ 24. Taylor hadn't ought to ask the bank to loan him money for a drum set.

_____ 25. Kim faces a dilemma about which of her new outfits to wear to the job interview plus she can't decide which drawings to take.

CHAPTER 17   SYMBOLS FOR CORRECTING THEMES

Abbreviations
Spell out this word.

ab

Most teachers discourage the use of abbreviations in formal writing. The ones listed below, however, are permissible:
- Before personal names—Dr., Mr., Mrs., Messrs., St.
- After personal names—Sr., Jr., Esq., M.A., Ph.D. (and other academic degrees)
- After time of day—A.M., P.M.
- Before dates—A.D.
- After dates—B.C.
- Before numerals—No.
- In scientific writing—rpm, mph, amp (and other units of measurement)
- FBI, NATO, UNESCO, CBS, NBC, TVA, NASA (and other companies, institutions, and agencies). Note that the periods in these abbreviations are commonly omitted.

Abstract terms
Substitute a concrete expression for this term.

abst

Abstract words often lead to wordiness and misinterpretation. Wherever possible, try to use concrete words which name things that can be seen, touched, smelled, tasted, or heard.

Adjective
Change this word to an adjective.

adj

Linking verbs (which say the subject *is* something rather than that it *does* something) are usually followed by adjectives, not adverbs. Linking verbs include such words as *be, seem, become, appear, prove,*

109

remain, look, sound, feel, taste, smell, (and more rarely) stay, turn, go, and grow.

    I feel badly today. (Faulty)
    I feel bad today. (Correct)

    The hat looks well on you. (Faulty)
    The hat looks good on you. (Correct)

    The flower smells sweetly. (Faulty)
    The flower smells sweet. (Correct)

    The corn grows straightly. (Faulty)
    The corn grows straight. (Correct)

Adverb
adv

Change this word to an adverb.

    The party was real enjoyable. (Faulty)
    The party was really enjoyable. (Improved)
    The party was very enjoyable. (Better still)

    Both Tim and Margie dance good. (Faulty)
    Both Tim and Margie dance well. (Correct)

Agreement
agr

Change one or more of the words indicated to make certain that (1) verbs agree with subjects in number, (2) pronouns agree with antecedents in number, gender, and person, and (3) adjectives agree with nouns in number.

1. *Subjects and verbs must agree in number.*

    Either Pat or Don are coming Monday. (Faulty)
    Either Pat or Don is coming Monday. (Correct)

    Either Pat or the children are coming. (Correct—verb agrees with nearer subject in either-or sentence)
    Either the children or Pat is coming. (Correct—verb agrees with nearer subject in either-or sentence)

    One of the men on the stage crew handle the lights. (Faulty)
    One of the men on the stage crew handles the lights. (Correct)

    This is one of the books which collects dust. (Faulty)
    This is one of the books which collect dust. (Correct)

2. *Pronouns and antecedents must agree in number, gender, and person.*

    Each senior must return their keys before Wednesday. (Faulty number)
    Each senior must return his (her) keys before Wednesday. (Correct)

    All students will have her (his) turn in the Home Living Center. (Faulty number)

Symbols for Correcting Themes

>All students will have their turns in the Home Living Center. (Correct)

>The speaker gave us its opinion on fiscal policy. (Faulty gender)
>The speaker gave us his opinion on fiscal policy. (Correct)

>The cow offers milk in exchange for his board and keep. (Faulty gender)
>The cow offers milk in exchange for her board and keep. (Correct)

>When anyone goes on a hike, you should take a good compass. (Faulty person)
>When anyone goes on a hike, he (she) should take a good compass. (Correct)

>I like to take afternoon naps, but you shouldn't do it too often. (Faulty person)
>I like to take afternoon naps, but I shouldn't do it too often. (Correct)

3. *An adjective must agree with its noun in number.*
   Sherm dislikes these kind of programs. (Faulty)
   Sherm dislikes this kind of program. (Correct)
   Sherm dislikes these kinds of programs. (Correct)

   Students must not park their car in the faculty lot. (Faulty)
   Students must not park their cars in the faculty lot. (Correct)

Ambiguity

amb

Rewrite this sentence to eliminate ambiguity.

Intentional ambiguity, in which the writer hopes to force the reader to select between alternative meanings, is extremely rare in professional writing and almost nonexistent in student papers. When the writer's thoughts are not being expressed clearly, unintentional ambiguity may result either from fuzzy thinking or from awkward sentence constructions such as the following:

>The church is one of the most important institutions in our society. They provide social as well as spiritual support. (Ambiguous)
>The church, which provides social as well as spiritual support, is one of the most important institutions in our society. (Clear)

>Abby told Robin that her mother was sick. (Ambiguous)
>Abby told Robin that Abby's mother was sick. (Clear)

Apostrophe

ap

Insert apostrophe where indicated.

Use an apostrophe to indicate the following: (1) the possessive case of nouns and indefinite pronouns, and (2) omissions of letters.

1. *Use an apostrophe to show possession of nouns and indefinite pronouns.*
    a. Any noun that does not end in *s* forms its possessive with an apostrophe and an *s*.
        man's hat   (singular)
        men's hats   (plural)
    b. Any plural noun that does end in *s* forms its possessive with an apostrophe after the *s*.
        ladies' dresses
        monkeys' paws
        the Joneses' lawn
        the Browns' house
    c. A singular noun ending in *s* forms its possessive either with an apostrophe and an *s* or with the apostrophe alone. If the word is very long or if the addition of another *s* leads to difficulties of pronunciation, the simple apostrophe is preferable.
        Short singular nouns (easy to pronounce)
            Keats' poems
            Keats's poems
            Jesus' parable
            Jesus's parable
        Long singular nouns (difficult to pronounce)
            Diogenes' quest
            Dionysius' festival
    d. An indefinite pronoun forms its possessive with an apostrophe and an *s*.
        someone's gloves
        nobody's champion
        everybody's choice
        another's opinion
    Note that personal pronouns never take an apostrophe to show possession.
        The election is ours.
        The committee demanded its rights.
        The decision is hers.
        Is this sweater yours?

2. *Use apostrophes to indicate omissions of letters.*
    a. The apostrophe takes the place of letters omitted in contractions.
        I don't (do not) want any excuses.
        I shouldn't (should not) permit any interference.
        I'm (I am) planning to arrive by 7 o'clock (of the clock).
    b. The apostrophe takes the place of sounds omitted in speech.
        It takes a heap o' livin' to make a house a home.

awk *k*

Awkward
Rewrite this material, which is awkwardly expressed.

Symbols for Correcting Themes

Big word
Use a simple word instead of this big one.

Big w

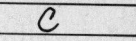

Comma
Insert a comma at the place indicated, or substitute a comma for the mark of punctuation used.

C

Twelve general rules govern the use of commas:

1. *Use a comma before the coordinating conjunction which joins two independent clauses.*
    I wanted to see the movie, but no one would go with me.

2. *Use commas between items in a series.*
    Last year I studied history, mathematics, and art.

3. *Use a comma between coordinate adjectives preceding a noun.*
    Have you ever longed for a carefree, unplanned vacation? (To test if the adjectives are coordinate, try placing an *and* between them. If the *and* does not sound natural, do not use a comma.)

4. *Use a comma after an introductory modifier.*
    When the meeting was finally called to order, half the committee members had already left. (Introductory adverbial clause)
    Having already ordered a hamburger, I did not think I could eat the salad the waitress brought. (Introductory participial phrase)
    In spite of Marilyn's poor coordination and lack of self-confidence, she has entered the tournament every year. (Long introductory prepositional phrase. Short prepositional phrases do not require commas.)

5. *Use a comma to set off words and phrases that may be misread.*
    Once inside, the cat licked its paws.

6. *Use commas to set off nonrestrictive clauses and phrases.* When a noun or pronoun is already completely identified by a proper name or some adjective, the clause or phrase which further modifies it is nonrestrictive. It is *added information* and calls for commas.
    Professor Clawson, who teaches my speech class, gives silly assignments. (Identified by name)
    My mother, knowing my fondness for crab, fixed a delicious seafood casserole. (Only one mother—fully identified)
When a noun or pronoun relies upon a clause or phrase for identification, that clause or phrase is restrictive. It provides *essential information* and is not set off by commas.
    The professor who teaches my speech class gives silly assignments.
    Someone knowing my fondness for crab fixed a delicious seafood casserole.

7. *Set off appositives with commas.*
>Sharon, our neighbor, never rings the doorbell when she comes over.

8. *Set off absolute phrases with commas.*
>The barbecue is set, weather permitting, for Tuesday at 7 P.M.

9. *Set off parenthetical expressions with commas.*
>Bonnie, you will remember, has been hospitalized since June.

10. *Set off the name of the person spoken to with commas.*
>Charles, will you please wash the car before you use it this evening?
>
>Brush your teeth, Joan, if you don't want to get cavities.

11. *Set off the name of the speaker in dialogue with commas.*
>"Gee," said Bill, "why can't I go?"

12. *Set off more than one item of dates and addresses from the remainder of the sentence with commas.*
>Write to her at 125 Magazine Street, Cambridge, Massachusetts, before May 10.
>
>On July 5, 1946, my parents were married in Logan.

Case of pronoun
Change this pronoun for one in the correct case.

Personal pronouns and the pronoun *who* take different forms (spellings), depending upon their use in a sentence. The three cases of pronouns are nominative, objective, and possessive.

	NOMINATIVE	OBJECTIVE	POSSESSIVE
singular			
first person	I	me	my, mine
second person	you	you	your, yours
third person	he	him	his, his
	she	her	her, hers
	it	it	its, its
plural			
first person	we	us	our, ours
second person	you	you	your, yours
third person	they	them	their, theirs
	who	whom	whose

1. *Use the nominative case for (a) a subject of a verb or (b) a subjective complement.*
    a. Subject of a verb
    >I hoped that he would come.
    >
    >She was angry because he was late.

    Be careful to use the nominative form in comparisons after the conjunctions *as* and *than* when the pronoun is the subject of an understood (elliptical) verb.

I was sicker than he. (I was sicker than he was.)
Are you as hungry as I? (Are you as hungry as I am?)
Remember to use the nominative form when the pronoun subject is followed by a parenthetical expression like *I think* or *do you believe.*
Who do you believe will win the tournament?
Do not be misled by a preposition or verb which precedes a pronoun subject.
THE CASE OF A PRONOUN IS ALWAYS DETERMINED BY ITS USE WITHIN ITS OWN CLAUSE.
I will award the car to whoever holds the lucky number. (Whoever is the subject of the verb *holds.*)
The committee will decide who will be the guest of honor. (Who is the subject of *will be.*)

  b. Subjective complement
It was I who forgot your birthday.
Is this he speaking?

2. *Use the objective case for* (a) *a direct object,* (b) *an indirect object,* (c) *an object of a preposition, or* (d) *the subject of an infinitive, whether the infinitive is expressed or understood.*
   a. Direct object
   I pinched him.
   Then he kicked me.
Remember, however, that when *whom* is the object of a verb, it will come at the beginning of the clause, not after the verb.
Whom did you hire for the Albany office?
Rachel is a girl whom everyone admires.
   b. Indirect object
   Uncle Ted read her a story.
   Dad bought me a car.
   c. Object of a preposition
   Uncle Ted read a story to her.
   Dad bought a car for me.
   d. Subject of an infinitive
   I hated him to be late.
   The audience coaxed her to sing another number.
   Mother made me work. (The *to* of the infinitive *to work* is understood.)

3. *Use the possessive case to show ownership.*
   Is this your sweater?
   Is this sweater yours?
Use the possessive case to show ownership of abstract concepts expressed in gerunds.
   I question his winning the election honestly.
   I am counting on your attending the meeting.
   His jumping out the window was stupid.

The most common problems with case forms occur (1) when pronoun objects are separated from their prepositions or verbs and (2) when pronouns are joined with nouns or other pronouns.
1. Pronoun objects separated from their prepositions or verbs.
    Whom did you speak to? (Very formal)
    Him I shall marry.
2. Pronouns joined with nouns or other pronouns.
    The Aquamaids invited Ms. Standish and me to serve as coaches.
    Just between you and me, the demonstration was a bore.
    The only ones present were she and I.
    Dad lent the money to her and me.

Capital

`Cap`

Substitute a capital for the lowercase letter indicated.

Use capital letters in the following situations:

1. *Capitalize the first word of a sentence or of a direct quotation.*
    Rising to his feet, Tom said, "Your claim is utterly false."
   However, do not capitalize the second half of a quotation interrupted by some expression like *he said*.
    "Your claim," Tom said, rising to his feet, "is utterly false."
   Capitalize the second half of the quotation if it begins a new sentence.
    "Your claim is utterly false," said Tom. "It is dishonest and false."
   Do not capitalize indirect quotations.
    Tom said that Frank's claim was utterly false.
2. *Begin each line of traditional poetry with a capital letter.*

>   The gaudy, blabbing, and remorseful day
>   Is crept into the bosom of the sea.
>   Shakespeare, *II Henry VI*

3. *Capitalize proper nouns and most adjectives which come from proper nouns.*
    Andrew Jackson . . . Jacksonian spoils system
    Europe . . . European languages

4. *Capitalize titles of office only when they are used with names or when they stand alone for the person.*
    I want to talk to Professor Walker about my grade.
    The President of the United States will appear on television at 8:00 P.M.
    I want to talk to the professor about my grade.
    Gwen Anderson was just elected president of the Tri-State Club.

5. *Capitalize nouns showing family relationships but not when such nouns follow possessive nouns or pronouns or articles* (a, an, the).
    Stacy's mother is taller than Mother.
    My sister and I visited Aunt Sara in her office.
    Tell Grandmother she is not the only forty-year-old grandmother in the world.

Symbols for Correcting Themes

6. *Capitalize points of the compass when they refer to specific regions but not when they refer to direction.*
    My neighbor to the east went South for his health.

7. *Begin titles of books, short stories, poems, essays, and plays with a capital. Capitalize all other words in the titles except articles (a, an, the) and the short prepositions and conjunctions.*
    How to Read Better and Faster
    Leaves of Grass
    Good Housekeeping
    Reader's Digest
    Raisin in the Sun
    "Do Your Own Thing My Way"
    "Death of the Hired Man"

8. *Capitalize academic courses used with numbers.*
    I passed Chemistry 5 last term but failed history.

Comma Fault   `CF`

Insert a coordinating conjunction after the comma, or replace the comma with a semicolon or period.

The misuse of a comma between two independent clauses is known as a comma fault. This is a far more serious error than most punctuation errors involving commas.
    The committee meeting broke up after two hours, we could not come to an agreement. (Comma fault—serious error)

Separate two independent clauses in one of three ways: (1) a comma plus a coordinating conjunction, (2) a semicolon (with or without a coordinating conjunction), or (3) a period.

1. *Comma plus coordinating conjunction*
    The committee meeting broke up after two hours, for we could not come to an agreement.

2. *Semicolon (with or without a coordinating conjunction)*
    The committee meeting broke up after two hours; we could not come to an agreement.

3. *Period*
    The committee meeting broke up after two hours. We could not come to an agreement.

Better still than trying to punctuate the two independent clauses would be to change one of them to a subordinate construction.
    The committee meeting broke up after two hours *because we could not come to an agreement.* (Dependent clause)
    Having failed to reach agreement, we broke up the committee meeting after two hours. (Participial phrase)

Clarity   `Cl`
Rewrite and clarify this passage.

Coh

Coherence
Rewrite the passage indicated to make it cohere.

Coherence is dependent upon

1. The logical arrangement of ideas so that one leads naturally to the next.
2. The use of transitions. (Words, phrases, sentences, or even paragraphs that act as bridges between different ideas. See pp. 15–18.)

Both elements are necessary and must work together.

Col

Colon
Insert a colon at the place indicated, or substitute a colon for the mark of punctuation you have used.

The colon (:) is a somewhat formal mark of punctuation which anticipates a list, quotation, announcement, or question of some kind. Do not, however, use the colon immediately after a verb.

> Invited to the party were the following: Mr. and Mrs. Jarvis, Dr. and Mrs. Stanley, Senator and Mrs. Thomas, Mr. Hughes, and Ms. Bowman. (Colon—correct)
>
> Invited to the party were Mr. and Mrs. Jarvis, Dr. and Mrs. Stanley, Senator and Mrs. Thomas, Mr. Hughes, and Ms. Bowman. (No punctuation—correct)
>
> Invited to the party were: Mr. and Mrs. Jarvis, Dr. and Mrs. Stanley, Senator and Mrs. Thomas, Mr. Hughes, and Ms. Bowman. (Colon after verb—questionable)

Edward Young once commented on the divine origin of the universe: "An undevout astronomer is mad." (Colon)
Edward Young said, "An undevout astronomer is mad." (Comma)

Comp

Comparison
Rewrite this sentence to eliminate faulty or incomplete comparison.

Faulty Comparisons

Mark Twain's humor appeals more to twentieth-century readers than most of his contemporaries. (Faulty)
Mark Twain's humor appeals more to twentieth-century readers than that of most of his contemporaries. (Correct)
Mark Twain's humor appeals more to twentieth-century readers than the humor of most of his contemporaries. (Correct)

The college gymnasium is larger than the high school. (Faulty)
The college gymnasium is larger than the high school's. (Correct)
The college gymnasium is larger than that of the high school. (Correct)
The college gymnasium is larger than the gymnasium in the high school. (Correct)

Incomplete Comparisons

Philosophy students are more concerned with the essential meaning of life. (Incomplete)

Symbols for Correcting Themes

>Philosophy students are more concerned with the essential meaning of life than are most members of the Establishment. (Complete)

Comma splice — *CS*
See ⎡ *CF* ⎦ above.
Revise sentence construction.

Construction — *Cst*
Revise sentence construction.

Diction — *D*
Change this word to one that is more precise in meaning or more appropriate in tone.

Dangling modifier — *Dang* *DM*
Revise sentence to eliminate dangling modifier.

Any modifier (i.e., a word or group of words functioning as an adjective or adverb) dangles if it has no word to modify in the same sentence. It is misplaced if it occurs in a sentence near a word which it could modify but does not. Because of the structure of English, you are seldom tempted to write sentences in which simple adjectives cause problems. Simple adverbs, however, are movable and therefore sometimes end up by the wrong word. More complex constructions cause more complex problems, some of which are listed below:

1. *Participles*
   The painting was entered in the Oakland Fine Arts Contest, *hoping for the $500 prize.* (Dangling)
   I entered the painting in the Oakland Fine Arts Contest, *hoping for the $500 prize.* (Misplaced)
   Hoping for the $500 prize, I entered the painting in the Oakland Fine Arts Contest. (Correct. The participle modifies the closest noun or pronoun.)

2. *Infinitives*
   To wash walls properly, the water should not be allowed to trickle down dirty surfaces. (Dangling)
   The water should not be allowed to trickle down dirty surfaces *to wash walls properly.* (Dangling)
   To wash walls properly, one should not allow the water to trickle down dirty surfaces. (Improved)

3. *Elliptical adverb clauses*
   An elliptical clause is one in which something important is understood—sometimes even the subject and verb. When the subject of the clause is understood, problems of structure may occur.
   When six years old, my father remarried.
   This sentence is obviously wrong. A man could not marry for the second time at age six. But how about this sentence?

When sixty years old, my father remarried.

Technically this sentence says that the father married for a second time when he was sixty years old. If the writer intended a different meaning, he is guilty of writing a dangling modifier. Here is the rule to follow: THE SUBJECT OF THE ELLIPTICAL CLAUSE MUST BE THE SAME AS THE SUBJECT OF THE EXPRESSED CLAUSE, OR THE ELLIPTICAL CLAUSE DANGLES.

When [I was] six years old, my father remarried. (The elliptical clause dangles because the subject of the two clauses are different.)

When [my father was] sixty years old, my father remarried. (The elliptical clause does not dangle because the subjects of the two clauses are the same.)

4. *Prepositional phrases*

After a sickness of two weeks, the house was a mess. (Dangling prepositional phrase)

After being sick for two weeks, the house was a mess. (Dangling prepositional phrase containing a gerund)

After I was sick for two weeks, the house was a mess. (Correct)

(Since all dangling modifiers are not equally confusing, a teacher may not call all to the attention of a student.)

Detail
Support generalization with concrete details. (See Chapter 6.)

Division
Divide this word correctly. See a dictionary.

Emphasis
Revise this passage to give emphasis to the most important idea.

Achieve emphasis by one of the following methods:
1. *Place the most important idea last.* (If that is impossible, place the most important idea first.)
2. *Repeat important words in a meaningful way.* (Avoid unconscious repetition, however.)
3. *Use balanced sentence constructions.*
4. *Avoid wordiness.*
5. *Use active verbs.*
   Passive verbs—weakest
   Linking verbs—stronger
   Active verbs without direct objects—stronger still
   Active verbs with direct objects—strongest

Figure of speech
Revise this figure of speech.

Figures of speech are words and phrases which carry meanings beyond their literal ones. Fresh and appropriate figures of speech give

Symbols for Correcting Themes

vitality to writing by providing valuable sensory impressions for a reader—things he or she can see, touch, hear, taste, and smell. But nothing gives away second-rate prose and poetry as quickly as ineffective figures of speech. Poor figures of speech are explained below:

1. *Mixed figures of speech* result when two or more unrelated concepts are combined in a single sentence or paragraph.
   One way to smoke out a crook is to give him enough rope to hang himself.

2. *Trite figures of speech* are those which have been borrowed so frequently they no longer have any luster or vigor.
   hungry as a bear . . . a ripe old age . . . a budding genius . . . fit as a fiddle . . . the sea of matrimony . . . proud as a peacock . . . her salad years . . . slippery as an eel

3. *Unnatural figures of speech* occur when the figurative expressions are too formal, too pompous, too humorous, too serious, too slangy, or too ridiculous for the passages in which they appear.
   Slowly, slowly Jake bent the iron bar, his huge biceps twitching like the wings of a butterfly balancing on a single blade of grass.

4. *Habitual figures of speech* weaken composition as would any good device used too frequently. As a general rule, however, similes are the most irritating of all figures of speech when they are overworked because the repeated sounds of *like* and *as* grind the ear even when the passages are read silently.

Fragment

Attach this fragment to an independent clause or revise it to stand alone.

Any group of words punctuated as a sentence but unable to stand alone is a fragment. Some fragments, such as bits of dialogue, responses to questions, and exclamations, are permissible in composition. But examine all intentional fragments to make certain that they could not be expressed better in other ways. The following errors are typical of *unintentional* student fragments:

1. *Verbal phrases*
   Apparently having enlisted for service some time during the course of the Vietnam war. (Fragment)
   Never to be considered for one of the college's dramatic productions. (Fragment)

2. *Dependent clauses*
   Whenever Sandra and Joel come to town for the Christmas holidays. (Fragment)
   Because history is not a required subject for nursing majors. (Fragment)

3. *Phrases beginning with the adverb* **especially**
   Especially during discussions of the pass-fail system.

Corrections
Apparently having enlisted for service some time during the course of the Vietnam war, Burns decided to make the army his career.

Never to be considered for one of the college's dramatic productions was painful for Tanya.

Whenever Sandra and Joel come to town for the Christmas holidays, they fail to bring all their children.

Because history is not a required subject for nursing majors, I never studied anything about the Civil War.

Fred shouted frequently during his meeting with the president, especially during discussions of the pass-fail system.

Glossary
See Glossary of Usage, p. 96.

Gobbledygook
Say this in plain English.

Relative to the supplication postulated in your missive of the 10th instant, we regret proffering notification of our permanently depleted inventory of Irish lace. (Foolish)

We regret that we no longer stock Irish lace, which you requested in your letter of August 10. (Direct)

Grammar
Revise sentence to eliminate error in grammar.

Hyphen
Insert hyphen at place indicated.

Idiom
Rewrite this expression. It is not idiomatic in English.

Illustrate
Illustrate the generalization with one or more examples. (See Chapter 7.)

Italics
Underline (place in italics) the material indicated.

Use italics for four purposes:

1. *Underline titles of books and periodicals.*
    Do you subscribe to *Time*?
    The Experience of Literature is an excellent textbook for introductory classes.
    I read in the *Chronicle* that the university received a $500,000 grant from the Ford Foundation.

2. *Underline foreign words and phrases.*
    After a while the debaters resorted to *argumentum ad hominem*.
    He claimed his invention was for *tout le monde*.

Symbols for Correcting Themes   123

3. *Underline an occasional word or phrase* (*for emphasis*).
   He finally admitted he had not eaten for *ten days!*
   Rawlings is the *only* candidate worth considering.

4. *Underline* (*or place in quotation marks*) *words used as words.*
   Russell just can't spell *all right.*

Awkward | *K* |
See | *awk* | above.

Lowercase | *lc* |
Do not use a capital letter.

Logic | *Log* |
Revise the logical relationship here.

Misplaced modifier | *mm* |
Revise sentence, putting misplaced modifier closer to the word it modifies.

For examples of dangling and misplaced modifiers, see above. | *Dang* | *DM* |

Mixed voice, mood, or construction | *Mx* |
Change one part of this sentence or passage to conform with the rest.
   After she saw the movie, the book was read. (Faulty)
   After she saw the movie, she read the book. (Correct)

   The cook must separate the white from the yolk. Beat the white first. (Faulty)
   Separate the white from the yolk and beat the white first. (Correct)

   By applying in March is usually the way to get a summer job. (Faulty)
   Applying in March is usually the way to get a summer job. (Improved)
   By applying in March one can usually get a summer job. (Better still)

No apostrophe | *no ap* |
Remove unnecessary apostrophe.

The use of apostrophes to indicate any plurals other than numbers, symbols, and words used as words is incorrect. Errors are frequently committed on doormats, mailboxes, and printed Christmas cards. The use of apostrophes with possessive personal pronouns is also incorrect.
   Merry Christmas from the Smiths'. (Faulty)
   Merry Christmas from the Smiths. (Correct)
   Merry Christmas from the Moss'. (Faulty)
   Merry Christmas from the Mosses. (Correct)

   Is this book your's? (Faulty)
   Is this book yours? (Correct)

The cat lay in it's basket. (Faulty)
The cat lay in its basket. (Correct)

No comma
Remove comma, or substitute the proper mark of punctuation for the comma here.

For comma rules, see ⌊ C ⌋ above.

No colon
Remove colon, or substitute the proper mark of punctuation for the colon here.

For colon rules, see ⌊ Col ⌋ above.

No paragraph
Do not indent here for new paragraph.

Omission
Supply the missing word or words.

Paragraph
Indent for new paragraph.

Paragraph coherence
See ⌊ Coh ⌋ above.

Paragraph unity
Stick to the controlling idea in the topic sentence. Paragraph lacks unity.

Passive
Change this passive verb into an active one.

In an active sentence the performer of the action is the subject of the verb. In a passive sentence the performer of the action is the object of a prepositional phrase (sometimes understood). As a rule, sentences in the active voice are more forceful and less wordy.

    The mail was awaited by me with great anxiety. (Passive—weak)
    I awaited the mail with great anxiety. (Active—improved)

    The boy was pummeled by his father. (Passive—weak)
    His father pummeled the boy. (Active—improved)

    The book was read aloud. (Passive—weak)
    He read the book aloud. (Active—improved)

Plural
Make this word plural.

Predication
Rewrite this sentence to eliminate faulty predication.

Symbols for Correcting Themes 125

    Norma's wealth, which all her neighbors envied, was the second book she wrote. (Faulty)

    Norma's wealth, which all her neighbors envied, came from the second book she wrote. (Correct)

    Jim's frustration in lending his gun to Joe was getting it back uncleaned. (Faulty)

    Jim's frustration in lending his gun to Joe was caused by getting it back uncleaned. (Correct)

Point of view   `PV`

Revise sentence to maintain a single point of view throughout the composition.

    I like to go on a long fishing trip every year. Camping is the only way you can get away from telephones and other problems of civilization. (Shift in point of view)

    I like to go on a long fishing trip every year. Camping is the only way I can get away from telephones and other problems of civilization. (Improved)

Question   `Ques`

Use a question mark here.

Quotation marks   `Quot`

Examine the sentence to insert quotation marks or to correct the punctuation used.

Use quotation marks for three purposes:

1. *Enclose directly quoted words in quotation marks.*

    "If you play that record one more time," said Grandma, "I'll scream."

    Three-year-old Kirk referred to the hostess as "the party's mother."

2. *Enclose words used as words in quotation marks.*

    Karen confused her "there's" and "their's" throughout the paper.

[Words used as words may also be set in italics. See `It`, No. 4.]

3. *Enclose titles of chapters, stories, poems, and articles published as **parts** of longer works in quotation marks.*

    I enjoyed reading "The Bean-Field" in *Walden*.

    Shirley Jackson's "The Lottery" appears in many anthologies.

    Have you read "Mending Wall"?

Relation of terminal punctuation to quotation marks:

1. Always place commas and periods inside quotation marks.

    "It requires a very unusual mind," says Alfred North Whitehead, "to undertake the analysis of the obvious."

    According to Addison, "Health and cheerfulness mutually beget each other."

2. Always place colons and semicolons outside quotation marks.
   The ambassador asked the waiter for a "few essential delicacies": fried eel, chocolate-covered ants, and bird's-nest soup.
   David was his father's "prodigal son"; but Mr. Stewart would do anything for that boy.

3. Place question marks and exclamation points inside the quotation marks if they belong to the quoted material or to both the quoted material and the outside sentence. Place question marks and exclamation points outside the quotation marks if they belong only to the sentence outside.
   Martha asked, "Are you coming?"
   Did Martha ask, "Are you coming?"
   Did Martha say, "I am coming"?

   Ernest shouted, "Get out of the street!"
   Stop saying "I won't!"
   Stop saying "She is light complected"!

Note that indirect quotations do not go in quotation marks.
   Her mother said that Kathy is lazy and indifferent.

Reference

Revise this sentence so that the pronoun reference will be perfectly clear and precise.
   Before Jan takes the dog for a walk, she should have a bath. (Foggy)
   The dog should have a bath before Jan takes her for a walk. (Clear)

   It said in the newspaper that new fighting had broken out in Jordan. (Careless)
   The newspaper said that new fighting had broken out in Jordan. (Precise)

   Motorcycles cause too many traffic accidents. Who needs them? (Foggy)
   Motorcycles cause something we don't need—traffic accidents. (Clear)

   At the supermarket they told me how to select good avocados. (Inexact)
   The produce manager at the supermarket told me how to select good avocados. (Precise)

Repetition

Revise sentence to eliminate weakening repetition.
   The pictures are framed in inexpensive frames. (Poor)
   The pictures are framed inexpensively. (Improved)

   Fascinated by gourmet food, Dan eats in every gourmet restaurant he can find. (Poor)
   Fascinated by exotic food, Dan eats in every gourmet restaurant he can find. (Improved)

Symbols for Correcting Themes

Run-on sentence
Separate the two independent clauses with a comma and coordinating conjunction, a semicolon, or a period.

A run-on sentence, in which two independent clauses are placed side by side with no punctuation between them, is probably the most serious punctuation error you can commit, even more serious than a comma fault, which is similar to it. See | *CF* | above.

Semicolon fault
Remove semicolon, or substitute the proper mark of punctuation for the semicolon here.

Do not use semicolons in place of commas, colons, or other marks of punctuation. There are only two ways in which you should use a semicolon:

1. *Use a semicolon (;) between independent clauses (with or without a coordinating conjunction).*
    Julian's first speech was well received; the other members of Congress rushed to congratulate him.
    Julian's first speech was well received; for the other members of Congress rushed to congratulate him.

2. *Use semicolons between items of a series when those items contain internal commas.*
    Last summer I visited Athens, Georgia; Moscow, Idaho; Oxford, Ohio; and Cairo, Illinois.

Shift
See | *Mx* | above.

Singular
Make this word singular.

Spelling error
Correct this misspelled word.

Spell out
Write out this number or clipped word.

Subordinate
Rewrite this material to subordinate one or more ideas.

Trite
Substitute an original expression for this trite one.

Trite expressions (overworked combinations of words) like the ones below demonstrate a writer's haste and emptiness of thought.

    last resort   worked like a Trojan
    high time   brown as a berry

blushing bride
majestic trees
sparkling eyes
crystal-clear water
this day and age
utmost importance
two left feet
peaches and cream complexion
strange bedfellows
today's modern world

apple of my eye
sight for sore eyes
best foot forward
cool as a cucumber
sober as a judge
soft as silk
stealthy as a cat
chip off the old block
high as a kite
stubborn as a mule

Trans

Transition
Provide a better transition between these two thoughts, sentences, or paragraphs.

Var

Variety
Revise this passage for greater variety in sentence construction.

VF

Verb form
Use the correct form of this verb.

 I should never have tore out the page. (Poor)
 I should never have torn out the page. (Correct)

 Marla drug her sister by the hand. (Poor)
 Marla dragged her sister by the hand. (Correct)

 The coat is laying on the bed. (Poor)
 The coat is lying on the bed. (Correct)

 Trudy set still for an hour. (Poor)
 Trudy sat still for an hour. (Correct)

Wdy

Wordy
Condense this passage for greater effectiveness. The idea expressed does not justify the number of words used.

WW

Wrong word
Find the right word, possibly one pronounced the same way but spelled differently.

✓

Delete
Delete the letter, letters, or material marked.

⌒

Close up
Close up this space.

/

Separate
Leave a space here.

?

Meaning
Meaning is not clear enough for the reader to understand.

Symbols for Correcting Themes 129

Parallelism
Rewrite this sentence to improve parallelism.

When putting sentence elements in a series or joining them with one of the seven coordinating conjunctions (*and, but, for, nor, or, so, yet*), express them in parallel form.
> Dan's jobs were to wash off the windshields, filling gas tanks, and general handyman. (Faulty)
>
> Dan's jobs were washing off windshields, filling gas tanks, and serving as general handyman. (Improved)
>
> Rhonda hoped to study French and that she could learn computer science. (Faulty)
>
> Rhonda hoped to study French and computer science. (Improved)

Conversely, do not use parallel constructions for ideas which are not logically parallel.
> Dennis is a first-string quarterback, serves as president of the student council, pops his gum noisily, and stars at track. (Misleading parallelism)
>
> Dennis, who unfortunately pops his gum noisily, is a first-string quarterback, serves as president of the student council, and stars at track. (Improved parallelism)

//

INDEX

Abbreviations
  correction symbol for misuse of, 109
Absolute phrases
  set off with commas, 114
Abstract idea,
  explained by analogy, 49
Abstract subject
  analyzed, 53
Abstract terms
  correction symbol for misuse of, 109
  defined for reader, 57
Accidental controlling ideas, 7
Accidental thesis statement, 78, 79
Ad, 97
Adjective
  correction symbol for, 109
Adverb
  correction symbol for, 110
Adverbial clauses
  comma after introductory, 113
Aggravate, 97
Agreement
  correction symbol for errors in, 110
Ain't, 97
All the farther, all the faster, 97
Almost, 97
Alright, 98
Ambiguity
  correction symbol for unintentional, 111
Among, between, 98
Analogies, 2
Analogy, 49–50
  defined, 49
  logical limitations of, 50
Analysis, 53–54
  defined, 53
And, but, for, nor, or, so, yet, 98
And etc., 98
Anecdote
  as conclusion, 90
  as introduction, 87
Anecdotes, 2, 27–28, 37
Antecedents
  agreement with pronouns, 110
Anyplace, anywheres, 98
Apology
  poor introduction, 88
Apostrophe
  correction symbol for, 111–12
  correction symbol for deletion of, 123
Appositives
  set off with commas, 114
Aren't, 98
Argumentative paragraphs, 15
Arrangement, logical, 6, 13, 18
As, 98
As, as if, as though, 98
At, 98
At about, 98
Auto, 98
Awful, awfully, 98
Awkward
  correction symbols for awkward constructions, 112, 123

Badly, 98
Balance, 99
Balanced sentence constructions
  for achieving emphasis, 120
Beautiful, 99
Because, 99
Beginnings
  (See Good Introductions and Poor Introductions)
Being as, being that, 99
Beside, besides, 99
Big word
  correction symbol for, 113
Blame on, 99
Brief dramatic incident
  good introduction, 87
Brief incident
  (See Anecdote)
But what, but that, 99

Cannot help but, 99
Capitalization
  correction symbol for, 116–17
Case of pronouns
  correction symbol for, 114–16
Categories
  dividing material into, 53–54
  overlapping and unbalanced, 54
Cause to effect order, 14, 15
Center around, 99
Central idea, 27
Character, 99
Chronological order, 23–25
Chronology, 14
Clarity
  correction symbol for, 117
Classification and differentiation
  definition by, 57, 58
Climactic order, 14–15, 54, 82, 89
Close up
  correction symbol for removing space, 128
Coherence, 13–18, 91–92, 118
  defined, 13, 91
  techniques for, 13
  in whole composition
Colon
  correction symbol for use of, 118
  correction symbol for deletion of, 124
Combination of methods of paragraph development, 71–72
Comma
  correction symbol for, 113
  correction symbol for deletion of, 124
Comma fault, 117
Comma splice, 119
  (See Comma fault)
Comparison, 118
  as transitional device, 91
Comparison and contrast, 43–45
  defined, 43
Comparisons
  faulty, 118
  incomplete, 118–19
Complected, 100
Complexity, order of, 14, 15
Composition, meandering and pointless, 78

Conclusion
    unnecessary with climactic order, 82, 89
Conclusions, poor, 91
Concrete detail
    (See Details)
Construction
    correction symbol for poor, 119
Contradictory thesis statements, 79–80
Contrast
    (See Comparison and Contrast)
Contrast which emphasizes thesis
    good introduction, 86
Contrasts
    analogy seldom concerned with, 49
Controlling idea, 7–8, 13, 72
Correcting themes
    symbols for, 109–29
Could not hardly, could not scarcely, 100
Could of, would of, might of, 100
Critique, 100
Cute, 100

Dangling modifier
    correction symbol for, 119
Dates
    set off with commas, 114
Definition, 57–60
    by anecdote, 57, 58
    by classification and differentiation, 57–58
    by comparison and contrast, 57, 59
    dictionary
        poor introduction, 88
    by exclusion, 57, 59–60
    by history, 57, 59
    by illustration, 57, 59
Delayed thesis introductions, 86–88
Delete
    correction symbol for material to be deleted, 128
Dependent clauses
    as sentence fragments, 121–22
Description, 5, 6
Descriptive paragraph, 6
Detail
    correction symbol for passage lacking sufficient, 120
    distinguished from illustration, 39
Details, 2, 6, 31–32, 39
    defined, 32
Diction
    correction symbol for inappropriate, 119
Dictionary definition
    poor introduction, 88
Died with, 100
Differences, 43
    (See also Comparison and Contrast)
Different than, 100
Dilemma, 100
Direct objects
    pronouns used as, 115
Disunified paragraphs, 7–8
Division of words
    correction symbol for improper, 120
Don't, 100

Echo of title
    poor introduction, 88

Editorials, 6
Effect to cause order, 14, 15
Effective composition, 31
Elegant, 101
Elliptical adverbial clause, dangling, 119–20
Emphasis
    correction symbol for faulty, 120
    short paragraph used for, 8
Emphatic order
    (See Climactic Order)
Endings
    (See Good Conclusions and Poor Conclusions)
Enthused, 101
Equally as good, 101
Every place, 101
Evidence, supporting, 78–80
Exam, 101
Example
    (See Illustration)
Examples, 2
Exclamation point
    use of with quotation marks, 126
Exclusion
    definition by, 57, 59–60
Exhortation
    poor conclusion, 91
Expect, 101
Explanation
    (See Exposition)
Explanation, process, 24–25
Explanatory paragraphs, 15
Exposition, 28
    defined, 5
Expository paragraph, 2, 5, 6
Expository purpose, 27
Extended definition
    (See Definition)

Facts, 63–65
    (See also Details)
Farther, further, 101
Faulty comparisons
    correction symbol for, 118
Faulty predication
    correction symbol for, 124
Fewer, less, 101
Figure of speech
    symbol for revision of, 120–21
    as transitional device, 91
Fine, 101
First-sentence thesis
    good introduction, 85
Flashback, 28
Foreign words and phrases
    use of italics for, 122
Fragment
    symbol for correction of, 121–22
Fun, 101

Gender
    agreement of pronouns and antecedents, 110–11
General statement
    (See Generalization)
Generalization, 3–4, 6, 31, 32, 37, 80
Gerunds
    use of pronouns with, 115

Index

Glossary of usage, 96–106, 122
Gobbledygook, 122
Good conclusions, 89–91
   anecdote, 90
   memorable restatement of thesis, 91
   quotation, 90
   solution for a problem presented in the composition, 90
   statement designed to make reader think or act, 90
   summary, 91
Good introductions, 85–88
   brief dramatic incident, 87
   contrast which emphasizes thesis, 86
   first-sentence thesis, 85
   question which leads to thesis, 86
   quotation, 88
   statement designed to startle reader, 87
   statement which anticipates reader's objections, 88
   statement which relates subject to topic of current interest, 87
Grammar
   symbol for correction of error in, 122
Grammatical errors, 18
Great, 101
Gym, 101

Habitual figures of speech
   symbol for correction of, 121
Hadn't ought, 101
Have got, 101
Heighth, 101
Hisself, theirselves, 102
Historical discussions, 14
History
   definition by, 57, 59
How come, 102
How-to-do-it paragraphs, 23–24
Hung, 102
Hyphen
   correction symbol for, 122
Idiom
   correction symbol for faulty, 122
Illustrate
   correction symbol to show need to, 122
Illustration, 37–39
   defined, 37
   distinguished from detail, 39
In the case of, in some cases, in this case, etc., 102
Incomplete comparisons
   correction symbol for, 118–19
Indefinite pronouns
   use of apostrophe with, 112
Independent clauses
   punctuation of
Indirect objects
   pronouns used as, 115
Indirect quotations
   no capitalization for, 116
   no quotation marks for, 126
Infinitives
   dangling, 119
   pronouns as subjects of, 115
Inflated declaration of commonplace idea
   poor introduction, 88

Informal outline, 81–82, 85
Inside of, 102
Introduction
   defined, 85
   long
      symptom of poor organization, 85
Introductions
   (See Good Introductions and Poor Introductions)
Introductory modifier
   punctuation of, 113
Irregardless, 102
Is when, is where, 102
Italics
   correction symbol for, 122

Judgments
   (See Reasoning)

Key terms
   repetition of, 15, 17
Key words
   (See Controlling Idea)
Kind, sort, 102
Kind of, sort of, 102
Knowledgeable, 102

Lab, 103
Lend, loan, 103
Levels of usage, 96
Like, 103
List
   of implied narratives, 38
Listless prose, weak and, 31
Logic
   symbol for correction of faulty, 123
Logical arrangement, 6, 13, 18
Logical limitations of analogy, 50
Lose out, miss out, win out, 103
Lots of, a lot of, 103
Lovely, 103
Lower case
   correction symbol calling for, 123

Meandering and pointless composition, 78
Meaning
   correction symbol for unintelligibility of, 128
Meaningless paragraphs, 31
Meaningless question
   poor introduction, 89
Memorable restatement of thesis
   good conclusion, 91
Misplaced modifier
   correction symbol for, 123
Mixed figures of speech
   correction symbol for, 121
Mixed voice, mood, or construction
   correction symbol for, 123
Most, 103

Names
   of persons spoken to set off with commas, 114
Narration, 5, 6, 27–28
Narrative paragraph, 6
Narratives, 14, 37–39
New information or problems
   poor conclusion, 91

News reporting, 5, 6
Newspaper paragraphs, 6
Nice, 103
No apostrophe
    symbol for deletion of apostrophe, 123
No colon
    symbol for deletion of colon, 124
No comma
    symbol for deletion of comma, 124
No paragraph
    symbol to indicate no indentation, 124
No place, 103
Nominative case of pronouns, 114
Nonrestrictive clauses and phrases
    punctuation of, 113
Noun, 18
Nowhere near, 103
Number, agreement in, 110

Object of preposition
    case of pronoun as, 115
Objective case of pronouns, 114
Off of, out of, 103
Omission
    correction symbol for, 124
Only, 103
Opinions, 63–67
Order, 13–15
    cause to effect, 14, 15
    climactic, 14–15
    of complexity, 14, 15
    effect to cause, 14, 15
    space, 6, 13, 14
    time, 6, 13, 14
Organization
    described in partition paragraph, 89
Outline, informal, 81–82, 85
Over with, 104

Paragraph
    symbol to indent for new, 124
Paragraph coherence
    symbol for correction of, 124
Paragraph, descriptive
    (See Descriptive paragraph)
Paragraph development, combination of methods for, 71–72
Paragraph, expository
    (See Expository Paragraph)
Paragraph, newspaper
    (See Newspaper Paragraph)
Paragraph, no
    symbol to indicate no indentation, 124
Paragraph unity, 5–8
    symbol for correction of, 124
Paragraphs, how-to-do-it, 23–24
Parallel constructions, 15, 18
Parallelism
    symbol for correction of poor, 129
Participles, dangling, 119
Particulars
    (See Details)
Partition paragraph, 89
Passive
    symbol for revision of passive verb, 124
Period
    in correction of comma fault, 117
    use with quotation marks, 125

Person
    agreement of pronouns and antecedents, 110
Personal pronouns, 112, 114
Phone, 104
Photo, 104
Phrases beginning with *especially,* 121–22
Plan
    informal outline as, 85
Plan on going, 104
Plural
    symbol for change of singular word to plural, 124
Plus, plus the fact, 104
Point of view
    correction symbol for awkward shift in, 125
Pointless composition, 78
Poor conclusions, 91
Poor introductions
    apology, 88
    dictionary definition, 88
    inflated declaration of commonplace idea, 88
    meaningless question, 89
    sentence which echoes the title, 88
    uninteresting announcement of paper's intent, 89
Possessive case of pronouns, 112, 114
Preaching
    poor conclusion, 91
Predication
    symbol for correction of faulty, 124–25
Prejudice, use, 104
Prepositional phrases, dangling, 120
Pretty near, pret' near, 105
Process, 23–25
Process explanation, 24–25
Pronoun, case of, 114–16
Pronouns, 15, 17–18
Prose illustration, 37–39
Prose, weak and listless, 31
Put in for, 105

Question
    symbol indicating need for question mark, 125
Question, meaningless
    poor introduction, 89
Question which leads to thesis
    good introduction, 86
Quotation
    as conclusion, 90
    as introduction, 88
Quotation marks
    symbol to indicate omission of or error in using quotation marks, 125–26

Reason is because, reason is on account of, 105
Reasoning, 63–67
    cause to effect, 64, 66–67
    defined, 63
    effect to cause, 64, 66
    problem to solution, 64, 65–66
    question to answer, 64–65
Refer back, 105
Reference
    symbol for correcting pronoun reference, 126
Repetition
    symbol for revising repetitious passages, 126
Repetition of key terms, 15, 17
Research papers, 31–32
Run-on sentence
    symbol for correction of, 127

Index

Same, said, such, 105
Semicolon fault
   symbol for correction of, 127
Sentence which echoes the title
   poor introduction, 88
Separate
   symbol to indicate the need for a space, 128
Shift
   symbol to indicate awkward shift in voice, mood, tense, or construction, 127
Show up, 105
Similarities, 43
   (See also Comparison and Contrast)
Similarity
   analogy concerned with, 49
Singular
   symbol for correction from plural to singular, 127
So, such, 105
Solution for a problem presented in the composition
   good introduction, 90
Some, 105
Some place, someplace, 105
Space order, 6
Spelling error
   symbol for correction of, 127
Spell out
   symbol indicating need to, 127
Statement designed to make reader think or act
   good conclusion, 90
Statement designed to startle reader
   good introduction, 87
Statement, general
   (See Generalization)
Statement which anticipates reader's objections
   good introduction, 88
Statement which relates subject to topic of current interest
   good introduction, 87
Story, brief
   (See Anecdotes)
Subject
   difference between subject and thesis, 76–77
   of an infinitive
      case of pronoun as, 115
   of a verb
      case of pronoun as, 114
Subjective complement
   case of pronoun as, 115
Subordinate
   symbol for revising passage into dependent construction, 127
Summary
   good conclusion for long or technical papers, 91
   short paragraph used for, 8
   topic sentence as, 6, 91
Summary material, 85
Summary of paper
   thesis statement as, 85
Supporting evidence, 78–80
Supporting material, 85
Sure, 105
Suspicion, 105
Swell, 106

Symbols for correcting themes, 109–29
Synonyms and other substitutes, 15, 17

That there, this here, 106
Them, 106
Themes, symbols for correcting, 109–29
Thesis, 3
   difference between thesis and subject, 76
   fully developed, 89
   restatement of
      good conclusion, 91
Thesis beginnings, 85–86
Thesis statement, 76–82
   accidental, 78, 79
   incorporated in introduction, 78
   qualities of a good, 77
   as summary of whole paper, 85
Thesis statements
   contradictory, 79–80
Time order, 6, 21
Topic sentence, 3, 5, 6–8, 27, 38, 72, 76, 80, 91
Transition
   symbol for correction of inadequate, 128
   short paragraphs used for, 8
Transition sentence, 8
Transitional devices, 13, 15–18
Transitional paragraphs, 91
Transitional words and phrases, 15, 16–17, 18
Transitions, 72
   between paragraphs, 91–92
Tremendous, 106
Trite
   symbol for revision of trite passages, 127–28
Trite figures of speech, 121
Try and, 106

Uninteresting announcement of paper's intent
   poor introduction, 89
Unity, paragraph, 5–8
Unnatural figures of speech, 121
Usage, glossary of, 96–106
Usage, levels of, 96
Use, 106

Variety
   symbol for providing greater variety in sentence constructions, 128
Verb form
   symbol for correction of, 128
Verbal phrases, 121–22

Way, 106
Ways, 106
Weak and listless prose, 31
Where at, 106
Without, without that, 106
Wordy
   symbol for correcting wordy passages, 128
Would better, 106
Would have, 106
Wrong word
   symbol for correcting, 128